FORDHAM'S PERSONAL NARRATIVE

1817-1818

Fordham's
Personal Narrative
1817-1818

Travels in Virginia, Maryland, Pennsylvania, Ohio, Indiana, Kentucky; and of a Residence in the Illinois Territory

—by—

Elias Pym Fordham

—*with*—
Facsimiles of the Author's Sketches and Plans

Edited by
Frederic Austin Ogg, A.M.
Author of "The Opening of the Mississippi"

HERITAGE BOOKS
2011

HERITAGE BOOKS

AN IMPRINT OF HERITAGE BOOKS, INC.

Books, CDs, and more—Worldwide

For our listing of thousands of titles see our website
at
www.HeritageBooks.com

A Facsimile Reprint
Published 2011 by
HERITAGE BOOKS, INC.
Publishing Division
100 Railroad Ave. #104
Westminster, Maryland 21157

International Standard Book Numbers
Paperbound: 978-1-55613-196-7
Clothbound: 978-0-7884-8615-9

CONTENTS

ILLUSTRATIONS

EDITOR'S PREFACE

FOR information regarding the personal history of Elias Pym Fordham, author of the narrative herewith published, the Editor is indebted to Dr. Hubert de Laserre Spence, of Cleveland, Ohio, who has supplied not only a statement of his own knowledge of the enterprising young Englishman, but also a memorandum by his aunt, Sophia Worthington, and an interesting manuscript embodying the recollections of Mary Spence, his mother.

The preparation of the notes has been facilitated to such a degree by recent volumes of *Early Western Travels,* 1748-1846, edited by Dr. Reuben Gold Thwaites, that special acknowledgment of obligation ought to be made for use of material in the early volumes of travel made accessible in that valuable series. Full titles of the works chiefly referred to will be found in the list of contemporary travels at the end of this volume. It is hoped that the publication of the Fordham manuscript may be of service to students of Western history in general, and especially to those interested in the processes by which the composite population of the Mississippi Valley was built up in the great era of migration.

F. A. O.

HARVARD UNIVERSITY, January, 1906.

EDITOR'S INTRODUCTION

THE years immediately following the close of the second war with Great Britain witnessed a remarkable increase in the population of the Mississippi Valley, particularly of the old Northwest Territory and the remoter regions of Missouri and Arkansas. Aside from the high birth-rate uniformly characteristic of American frontier communities, this increase was due to an unprecedented influx of settlers from two sources: the seaboard states and Europe, chiefly Great Britain and Germany.

Prior to about 1815 emigration from the East to the West had been large in the aggregate, but very unsteady. The westward movement had been in the nature of successive waves separated by intervals of comparative inactivity. Three important epochs of migration since the establishment of national independence can be distinguished: (1) the years of uncertainty and distress between the end of the Revolution and the adoption of the Constitution; (2) the period including the "hard times" of 1800 and culminating in the acquisition of the Louisiana Territory in 1803; and (3) the era of commercial depression which began with the embargo of 1807 and continued until relieved by the succeeding war. During each of these periods of unsettlement, thousands of people in the older states abandoned conditions which they found disadvantageous, or positively onerous, and yielded to the allurements of the far-famed West. As time went on, the numbers increased and the movement tended steadily to become more constant and less dependent upon prosperity or the lack of it on the seaboard.

The outbreak of war in 1812, with the accompanying Indian uprisings in the West, checked the flow of homeseekers temporarily; but by the winter of 1814 the exodus from the East along the highways of New York and Pennsylvania and down the Ohio had come to be on such a scale as to call forth astonished comment in all sections of the country. By 1816 Ohio, which the census of 1810 showed to contain a population of 230,000, was estimated to be the home of 400,000 whites. In these six years the population of Indiana increased from 24,000 to 70,000, enabling this territory in 1816 to become a member of the federal union. From 406,000 to more than 500,000 was Kentucky's growth in the same period. And Illinois was brought from 13,000 or 14,000 almost to the attainment of statehood. The frontier — technically defined as the line of at least two settlers to the square mile, though more properly to be regarded as a belt or zone than as a line — was pushed back rapidly and given long finger-like protrusions up the larger water-courses, especially the Wabash, the Kaskaskia, the Mississippi, the Missouri, the Arkansas, and the Red.

In the Eastern states, where there was a strong disposition to lament the draining off of the sturdiest elements of the population, it was expected that the end of the war and the restoration of commercial prosperity (together with the rise of new and profitable industries) would reduce emigration across the Alleghenies to something like its earlier volume. But this anticipation was not realized. With each succeeding year after the Peace of Ghent the number of emigrants rose to a higher figure, and as a matter of fact the decade from 1815 to 1825 became the period during which the central Mississippi Valley attained its highest per cent of increase in population in the century. Land-hunger, dislike of overcrowding, discontent with economic conditions, love of adventure and novelty — these were the great forces which impelled men to forsake New England, New York, and Virginia for the ruder but roomier prairies and river-valleys of the West. The final suppression of the Indians, by William Henry Harrison in the Northwest and by Jackson in the South, relieved many prospective emigrants of the fears which had hitherto been an insuperable obstacle; and the development of steam navigation on the western lakes and rivers, which began with the launching of the "New Orleans" on the Ohio in 1811, provided means of travel and trade distinctively stimulative to migration and settlement.

The peopling of the West, however, was not left entirely to be accomplished by the migrations of native Americans. The same decade which was marked by so considerable a westward movement from the seaboard states was likewise notable for the unprecedented immigration of Europeans, part of whom settled in the East and offset in a measure the depopulation caused by the westward exodus, but a very large proportion of whom pressed on across the mountains in quest of homes in the fertile and undeveloped interior. Prior to 1820 no records of immigration were kept by the United States Government, and hence we have nothing better than unofficial estimates from which to judge the extent of the settlement of Europeans in America during the six important years following the Peace of Ghent. Since the majority of immigrants in this part of the century came from Great Britain, the hostilities of 1811-1814 very naturally caused a marked cessation in the movement. But about 1817 the tide resumed with greater force than ever, and in that year the total number of immigrants arriving was estimated at over 20,000. The number the following year was probably about the same. Congress saw in these figures a necessity for legislation to regulate the transportation of immigrants and to prevent the overcrowding of ships on which they made the voyage to the United States; and a law was enacted, March 2, 1819, containing suitable provisions in this direction and prescribing that an official count should begin to be kept the following year. The first records obtained in consequence of this legislation showed how overwhelmingly our immigrants from the United Kingdom outnumbered those from other European countries. While from September, 1819, to September, 1820, the number of Germans coming to the United States was but 948, of Frenchmen but 371, and of Spaniards but 139, that of British and Irish was 6,000.

The close of the Napoleonic wars left Great Britain in a condition, politically and economically, exceedingly favorable to heavy emigration. The nation had been engaged in a titanic conflict which had lasted with little intermission for more than twenty-two years and which had left the Government staggering under a war debt of £831,000,000. During this long period the movement for larger popular liberty, which had grown to considerable proportions during the years in which the seeds of revolution were ripening in France, had been held in abeyance; much had been lost in this time and nothing gained by the cause of liberalism. The Tory ministry, absorbed wholly in the conflict with the ambitious Corsican, had shown itself quite indifferent to domestic well-being and in the hour of victory its proud and complacent attitude betokened the period of political reaction through which England was destined in the next decade to pass. The establishment of a lasting peace cleared the way for a revival of domestic problems, and a great mass of discontented people who had been patriotic enough to withhold their criticisms while the nation was in danger, now became more insistent than ever that numerous and far-reaching reforms in governmental and industrial conditions be speedily undertaken.

2

Part of the evils complained of were political. Owing to excessive property requirements for the exercise of the franchise and the lack of adjustment of representation to the distribution of population, Parliament was very far from constituting a true national assembly and its legislation was felt to be that of a class for a class, regardless of the interests of the masses of the people. The multiplying of sinecure offices, created and maintained at heavy public expense for the benefit of do-nothing aristocrats, was regarded as another crying political abuse. Even more critical were the evils of an economic character. England was yet in the throes of the Industrial Revolution, and thousands of men were being crowded out of employment, temporarily at least, by the introduction of machinery and the establishment of the factory system. Then the return of peace reduced the foreign demand for many kinds of manufactured goods, resulting in a yet further over-supply of labor. The Corn Law of 1815, enacted for the express purpose of keeping up the price of food-stuffs, in the interest of the aristocratic landlord class, bore intolerably on the poverty-stricken tenants, and indeed upon the entire laboring class of the realm. The condition of the poor, in both city and country, was worse, relatively if not absolutely, in 1815 than it had been thirty years before. Wages which fell below the cost of bare subsistence coupled with rising rents and famine prices for bread could but stir up the spirit of insurrection; for economic distress will frequently provoke men to action when political disabilities call forth only harmless complaint.

The result was a period of incessant agitation for reform — for the liberalizing of the Government so that laws might be made according to the desires of the majority of the people, for the immediate repeal of obnoxious class legislation like the Corn Law, and for the cutting off of aristocratic sinecures and every other excrescence which made the burdens of the ordinary people harder to be borne. Led by William Cobbett, editor of the *Weekly Political Register,* Major John Cartwright, and others, the liberal element (organized into the Radical Party in 1819) entered upon a campaign which soon stirred the whole population and caused the Government to take stern measures to prevent the growth of the disaffection. Riots and popular demonstrations of every character became common and on several occasions — notably the gathering at Spa Fields, London, in 1816, and the Manchester Massacre (or "battle of Peterloo") in 1819 — the assemblies of the people to protest and organize against the existing state of things were forcibly broken up.

Success was destined to reward the agitators, but not until after many years and in many cases in ways quite different from those they had mapped out. In the meantime, during the period from about 1815 to 1820, while the movement was yet young and far from promising, many men became discouraged or impatient and sought the relief in emigration which they could see little reason to hope for if they remained in their old homes. "A nation," declared one of these, "with half its population supported by alms, or poor-rates, and one fourth of its income derived from taxes, many of which are dried up in their sources, or speedily becoming so, must teem with emigrants from one end to the other: and, for such as myself, who have had 'nothing to do with the laws but to obey them,' it is quite reasonable and just to secure a timely retreat from the approaching crisis — either of anarchy or despotism." About 1817-18 the desire to emigrate spread over the entire country and affected all classes of people except the privileged aristocrats. The land to which men looked for a new home, one which would be free from the oppressions of an aristocratic government and the distress occasioned by its economic policies, was quite naturally the United States. In the first place its population was made up predominantly of English-speaking people, bound to English people everywhere by numerous ties of sentiment and interest. In the next place it had at its disposal a superabundance of the choicest of land, which it was ready to bestow at inconsiderable cost. Even in the Eastern states land could be had at reasonable rates, and beyond the Alleghenies, especially in Indiana, Illinois, and to the westward, it need only be entered according to legal process and paid for within four years at the rate of two dollars an acre. Finally, the rapidly expanding manufactures of the United States, created largely during the war period, called for thousands of skilled laborers, so that English mechanics and artisans could expect to find profitable employment without being compelled to resort to the unaccustomed occupation of agriculture.

As a consequence of discouraging conditions at home and liberal advertising of the opportunities offered in America, emigration became easily the most discussed subject of the times, aside from the transcendent question of reform. That the actual migration in the years after 1815 was large is abundantly attested, not only by fragmentary evidences in contemporary American records, but also by the files of all the important English newspapers and magazines of the period. On the one hand, accounts of popular meetings in the interest of emigration to America are abundant, and on the other innumerable editorials and articles bewail the departure of the tillers of the soil, and also of not a few capitalists, for an alien country. The press made a united demand upon Parliament to stop the "ruinous drain of the most useful part of the population of the United Kingdom," and all manner of arguments, including many palpable falsehoods, were brought forth to dissuade men from migrating. But it was to no avail. People came from all parts of the kingdom, both country and city, to the ports to take passage. We are told that 229 English immigrants landed at New York in a single week, and that in the week ending Au-

gust 23, 1817, 1500 arrived at the five ports of
New York, New London, Perth Amboy, Philadelphia, and Boston. Nor were the immigrants all,
or even generally, of the poorest class. English law
forbade vessels to carry more than two passengers
for each ton, and this restriction was in itself sufficient to keep passenger rates at a high figure and
to preclude the pauper class from taking passage.
This fact only increased the indignation of the
English press, since the people who migrated were
almost exclusively the fairly well-to-do who could
most ill be spared. In his *Sketches of America,*
published in London in 1819, Henry Bradshaw
Fearon tells us that by 1817, when he was deputed
by thirty-nine English families to visit the United
States and ascertain what portions of the country
were best adapted to settlement by Englishmen,
"Emigration had .   .   .   assumed a totally new
character: it was no longer merely the poor, the
idle, the profligate, or the wildly speculative, who
were proposing to quit their native country; but
men also of capital, of industry, of sober habits and
regular pursuits, men of reflection who apprehended
approaching evils; men of upright and conscientious
minds, to whose happiness civil and religious liberty
were essential; and men of domestic feelings, who
wished to provide for the future support and prosperity of their offspring."

While the controversy regarding the expediency
of the settlement of Englishmen in America was
raging, an enterprise of large moment was under-

taken by two gentlemen of wealth and influence living in the vicinity of London—Messrs. Morris Birkbeck and George Flower. This was the establishment of an agricultural colony in southeastern Illinois, in the portion of Edwards County which afterwards came to be known as the English Prairie. Morris Birkbeck (1763-1825) was a successful practical farmer of Quaker origin who very well represents the type of well-to-do middle class Englishmen in this period who were dissatisfied with conditions in England and saw little prospect of an early improvement. Happening, in 1816, to meet the American diplomat, Edward Coles, who was returning from a mission to Russia, he first got from him an authoritative idea of the vast extent of unoccupied lands in the Illinois country. After some reflection he determined to sell his estate near London, migrate to Illinois with his family, and there prepare the way for the establishment of a colony of discontented English country laborers. Doubtless he expected to better his own fortunes, but his project seems to have been shaped in no small degree by philanthropic considerations. Another English farmer of similar station, George Flower, was attracted by the scheme and decided to join his old friend in it. In the summer of 1816 Flower came out to America in advance to get a personal knowledge of the land and its people. He visited various sections of the country, including the West, and, returning to Virginia in the autumn, spent most of the winter with Thomas Jefferson at

Monticello. The following spring Birkbeck, with his family, landed at City Point, Virginia, and with Flower proceeded to the Illinois. A tract of 16,000 acres of unbroken prairie was in part purchased outright and in part designated to be taken up later, and on this it was planned to locate the prospective colonists. The purchase lay in Edwards County, which at that time embraced an immense area, extending almost from the Ohio to Upper Canada and including a portion of the present state of Wisconsin. The two promoters then began to build log huts, import furniture, and make other preparations for the influx of settlers. Reports of the most optimistic character were sent back to England, with the result that a new stimulus was given to emigration, though many of the persons thus attracted found land that suited them without going so far west as to the English Prairie.

In the same year in which the settlement was begun Birkbeck published a book under the title *Notes on a Journey in America from the Coast of Virginia to the Territory of Illinois, with Proposals for the Establishment of a Colony of English* (Philadelphia, 1817). The next year another book, *Letters from Illinois* (London, 1818), appeared from the same author. Both attracted widespread attention in England, and the English Prairie settlement became the center about which was waged the whole controversy over the expediency of emigration of English people to America. Birkbeck's writings represented emigration, particularly if directed to his section of Illinois, as an enviable escape from political oppression and economic ruin and a sure road to good fortune and happiness. Some of those, however, whom he induced to settle in the western country were keenly disappointed, and, embittered by ill-luck or the hardships of frontier life, sent back reports denouncing Birkbeck in no uncertain terms and asserting that, having been himself deceived in the character of the American interior, he was seeking to recoup himself by selling his lands to unsuspecting emigrants. The letters of the malcontents were seized upon and made use of with avidity by those who were laboring to restrain emigration, while on the other hand men who were satisfied with the Western settlement or who had interests involved in its prosperity, as warmly defended Birkbeck's project. The result was a veritable war of the newspaper writers and pamphleteers — a war in the first instance between two groups of English writers attacking and defending, respectively, the policy of emigration; and in its later phase between the English who satirized American conditions and the Americans who resented this procedure and declaimed vehemently against it. While the literary belligerents talked and wrote, the people continued to migrate. Adlard Welby, a conservative Englishman who made a tour of inspection in the West in 1819, very fairly summed up the situation when he said: "These favorable accounts [the writings of Birkbeck], aided by a period of real privation and discontent in Europe, caused emigration to increase ten-fold; and though various reports of unfavorable nature soon circulated, and many who had emigrated actually returned to their native land in disgust, yet still the trading vessels were filled with passengers of all ages and descriptions, full of hope, looking forward to the West as to a land of liberty and delight — a land flowing with milk and honey — a second land of Canaan."

The ablest attack upon the English Prairie scheme was made by William Cobbett, the noted Radical leader and pamphleteer, who, in 1818, published his *Year's Residence in the United States of America* (New York, 1818), by way of a reply to Mr. Birkbeck's books. Cobbett was not opposed to emigration from England in itself, but he savagely denounced Birkbeck and all others who sought to induce the emigrant to go beyond the Alleghenies in search of a home. His writing upon this subject was done at a farm in Long Island where he was living in virtual exile, with prosecution for political offenses hanging over him if he returned to British jurisdiction. It cannot be known definitely whether, as Birkbeck declared, he was practically bought up by Eastern capitalists to advocate the settling of immigrants in the seaboard states rather than on the western prairies, but in any case this was the policy he urged with uncompromising fervor. For information as to what really were the conditions at the English Prairie Cobbett made use of Thomas Hulme's *Journal made during a Tour in the Western Countries of America: Sept. 30, 1818 — August 7, 1819.* Hulme was an honest English farmer, strongly Radical in principles and a follower of Cobbett. On the whole his *Journal,* however, exhibits a favorable attitude toward the Birkbeck enterprise, and it was only by twisting its statements and utterly ignoring their real import that the vilifying pamphleteer could adapt them to his ends. Cobbett's attack, which was renewed in successive editions of his book and in other writings, brought the English Prairie settlement its highest measure of notoriety, though scarcely to its profit. Birkbeck kept up his side of the controversy in similar new editions and incidental effusions, and was not lacking in out-spoken supporters. Chief among these was Richard Flower, father of George Flower, who in 1818 sold his estate in Hertfordshire and joined his relatives and former neighbors in Illinois. In 1819 he published *Letters from Lexington and the Illinois, containing a Brief Account of the English Settlement in the Latter Territory, and a Refutation of the Misrepresentations of Mr. Cobbett* (London, 1819); and somewhat later *Letters from the Illinois, 1820, 1821. Containing an Account of the English Settlement at Albion and its Vicinity, and a Refutation of Various Misrepresentations, Those more particularly of Mr. Cobbett* (London, 1822). In 1821 John Woods, a well-to-do, practical, and observant English farmer who had but lately established a home in the West, published *Two Years'*

Residence in the Settlement on the English Prairie, in the Illinois Country, United States. This, like Flower's books, was a sane, honest description of the settlement, which contrasted markedly in these qualities with the glib criticisms of writers like Cobbett, and showed that if conditions and prospects were not quite so roseate as Birkbeck pictured them they were at least immeasurably better than the detractors would have people believe.

Other books of this period, written by English travelers and settlers and containing noteworthy descriptions of the English Prairie in particular or of the Illinois country in general, are: (1) Henry Bradshaw Fearon's *Sketches of America. A Narrative of a Journey of five thousand miles through the Eastern and Western States of America; with Remarks on Mr. Birkbeck's "Notes" and "Letters"* (London, 1819); (2) Adlard Welby's *Visit to North America and the English Settlements in Illinois, with a Winter Residence at Philadelphia* (London, 1821); (3) William Tell Harris's *Remarks made during a Tour through the United States of America during the years 1817, 1818, and 1819* (London, 1821); (4) James Flint's *Letters from America* (Edinburgh, 1822); (5) George W. Ogden's *Letters from the West, comprising a Tour through the Western Country, and a Residence of two summers in the States of Ohio and Kentucky* (New Bedford, 1823); and (6) William Faux's *Memorable Days in America: being a Journal of a Tour to the United States, principally undertaken* to ascertain, by positive evidence, the condition and probable prospects of British Emigrants; including accounts of Mr. Birkbeck's settlement in the Illinois (London, 1823). Of these six writers it may be added simply that Fearon was an agent sent out by thirty-nine English families to ascertain what parts of the United States were best adapted to settlement; Welby was a conservative farmer of the upper middle class, prone to display in his writings a degree of insularity and prejudice even beyond that displayed by the average English traveler of the time; Harris was a fair-minded student of agrarian questions who came to America "with a view to estimating the advantages the United States were represented to afford;" Flint was a Scotch economist who emigrated primarily to study prices, wages, land questions, and labor problems, but who found pleasure in observing and recording his impressions of all sorts of things having little connection with economics; Ogden was an agriculturist and traveler of much the same type as Harris; and Faux was another farmer whose object in visiting the United States was to investigate the advisability of English migration thither — a writer who, though of inferior grade, yet in his characteristic blunt and inelegant manner supplies much valuable information.

One of the party of nine which accompanied Birkbeck to America in the spring of 1817 was a young Englishman by the name of Elias Pym Fordham, author of the letters and journal herewith published.

The family to which Fordham belonged is among the oldest in Eastern England. The claim is made that its line of descent can be traced back with ease as far as the time of King Stephen. For eight centuries its ancestral estates in Hertfordshire and Cambridgeshire have passed from generation to generation, and they are today in the possession of a branch of its vigorous descendants. Elias Fordham, father of Elias Pym, was born in 1763, and at the age of twenty-one married Mary Clapton, one of the last descendants of an honorable old family which, among other distinctions, had furnished Elizabeth a lord chancellor. The elder Fordham is described as a lively, bright, and happy man, whose admirable character and gracious manner won for him a multitude of friends. He was educated to be a Trinitarian minister and for some years had charge of a congregation of that faith; but, suffering an attack of throat trouble, he decided after a time to abandon the ministry and to become a brewer. In the new occupation he was doing well, until one night while riding near his home his horse stumbled over a tipsy man who, when aroused, managed to mumble that "it was all along of Fordham's fine ale." The incident troubled the conscientious brewer and the upshot was that he gave over the business, retired to Gannock where he had some property and, renting a tract of land of his brother, spent the rest of his life as a farmer. During his later years he occupied much of his time with occasional preaching, though diligent study of his Bible had led him to reject the Trinitarian and to adopt the hitherto despised Unitarian creed. In those days Unitarianism was looked upon by people generally with horror; yet so exemplary and sincere a man was Fordham that, rank dissenter though he had become, the bishop of his diocese licensed the kitchen of the worthy farmer's residence as a place for public worship.

In 1808 Mrs. Fordham died, leaving two sons, Elias Pym and Charles, and five daughters, Anne, Maria, Catherine, Harriet, and Sophia. Elias Pym became a pupil of George Stephenson and while yet a young man developed into a capable and promising engineer. Despite his enviable prospects, however, he was seized with the fever for migration to America which spread over England about 1816 and instead of settling in the practice of his profession at home began to cast about for a chance to try his fortunes in the New World. The opportunity was speedily forthcoming. George Flower was an uncle of his by marriage, and when Flower decided to take part in Birkbeck's projected settlement in the Illinois, Fordham, who was then twenty-nine years of age, resolved to be one of the first members of the new colony. As has already been related, Flower came to America in 1816, in advance of the rest of the party. Fordham came with Birkbeck and his family early the next year. The vessel on which they took passage from Gravesend brought them to the James River, in Virginia, whence the Birkbecks continued their journey westward over the mountains to Pittsburg, traveling in a phaeton and a light Jersey wagon, and thence went on horseback across southern Ohio to Cincinnati. Fordham took charge of the equipment which was being transported to the new settlement, consisting mainly of farming implements and household furniture, and arranged for its transportation by water from Norfolk to Baltimore, thence overland to Pittsburg and down the Ohio River to Cincinnati, where the party was reunited and from whence it proceeded across southern Indiana to the site of the prospective colony.

One of the ladies who accompanied the expedition was Fordham's sister Maria, who, being in illhealth, had been sent to America in the hope that the change would prove beneficial. In the Wabash country she soon became acquainted with a Frenchman, Charles de la Serre, who was descended from a Huguenot family which had fled from France at the time of the Revocation of the Edict of Nantes and settled in Guernsey. La Serre had abandoned his English home for a life of travel and sport in the American wilderness and, when discovered by Flower, was spending his time with a band of Indians in the vicinity of the English Prairie. In a short time he and Maria Fordham were married; but the young wife was still an invalid and died a few years later. A daughter, born in July, 1823, was the mother of Dr. Hubert de Laserre Spence of Cleveland, through whose good offices it has been ınade possible to publish the documents contained in this book.

Elias Pym Fordham made an entry of land in the English Prairie, and, from the outset found abundant labors to occupy his time in surveying, investigating the quality of lands to be purchased, and assisting in the preparation of buildings, mills, etc., for the use of prospective settlers. William Faux, who visited the Prairie in November, 1819, tells us in his *Memorable Days in America* that he met Fordham and that the young emigrant "never means to return to England, except rich, or to be rich. If he fails here, he will turn hunter and live by his rifle on the frontiers." Concerning his actual fortunes in the new home we know little, but in any event his residence in America was comparatively brief. We hear of him while not yet a middle-aged man once more in England following his favored occupation of civil engineering. That he enjoyed a high reputation for skill and integrity is evidenced by his appointment as Engineer to the Cinque Ports — a position in those days of no small trust and responsibility. He is known also to have been employed by Stephenson in various technical undertakings of national importance.

Late in 1818 a member of the family in England made a transcript of portions of the letters and journals which Fordham had sent home during the past eighteen months from Illinois. The collection (which in recent years has come into the hands of Dr. Spence) was given the title, *Extracts from Let-*

3

ters written on a Journey to the Western parts of the United States, and during a residence in the Illinois Territory, By an English Farmer. Its authorship has been positively identified and though it does not appear in all cases to whom the individual letters were addressed this is not a matter of much importance; the names of the addressees were omitted by the transcriber because they were regarded as of no consequence to the reading public, and because the persons in question were still living and did not desire the notoriety of appearing by name if the letters were printed. As a matter of fact, though it was evidently in the mind of the transcriber to publish the manuscript thus prepared, no further steps, so far as we know, were ever taken toward this end.

In adding another to the already long list of published records of western travel in the early part of the nineteenth century it may not be amiss to call attention briefly to the character of the new material and the degree of value it possesses for the student of western history. The manuscript falls naturally into three parts: (1) a series of seven letters, written between May 18 and November 15, 1817, from as many different places in the West and on the way thither; (2) a journal of daily happenings on and about the English Prairie from December 7, 1817, to February 26, 1818; and (3) another series of ten letters, written between February 3 and October 30, 1818, chiefly from Kentucky, Cincinnati, English Prairie, and the Indiana settlements at Princeton and New Harmony. Following roughly the chronology of Fordham's experiences during the first eighteen months of his sojourn in America, the movements which he recounts and the topics which he discusses, may be indicated somewhat as follows: the land and people of Virginia, a voyage up the Chesapeake, a trip on the Pennsylvania Road from Baltimore to Pittsburg, the people of western Pennsylvania, the city of Pittsburg, the descent of the Ohio to Cincinnati by flat-boat, the land and people of southern Indiana, establishing the settlement at the English Prairie, hardships of the first winter, the surveying and entering of public land, prices, wages, and labor in the West, the classes of people on the frontiers, a trip through Kentucky to Cincinnati, the character of the Kentuckians, the city of Cincinnati, the Rappite settlement at New Harmony, and the prospects for English emigrants in the American interior.

As is explained in the Preface prepared by the transcriber of the letters, the author wrote under all the disadvantages incident to the life of the frontier settler and explorer. He made no attempt to relate his experiences or to describe the Western people and country in a systematic and thoroughgoing fashion. He probably had not the slightest idea that the hurried letters which he despatched to relatives and inquiring friends and the fragmentary journals which he kept for their amusement and instruction would ever be put in print—at least without having undergone considerable revision.

What we have in his writings is not a formal compendium of information, like Fearon's *Sketches* or Melish's *Travels* of an earlier date, but simply a personal narrative of life as an English immigrant found it, and learned to share it, in a favored region of the growing West. The claim of the manuscript to the dignity of source material for the study of Western history arises from its author's superior intelligence and training, his candor and utter artlessness, and his rather unusual opportunities for observation. The scientific trend of mind which his professional study had developed saved him from numerous errors of other writers and led him to a wholesome comprehension of the difficulty of describing a frontier people with entire fairness and accuracy. "I find it no easy task," he acknowledges frankly, "to write descriptions of manners and opinions. If individual pictures only be drawn, the inferences must be in part erroneous; and sketches of a more comprehensive nature are either loose and incorrect, or tame and unreadable." In the main, Fordham wrote cautiously and conservatively, confining himself pretty closely to what he had himself seen and giving the reader due notice when speaking merely from hearsay. His only object was to keep his relatives and friends informed concerning his novel experiences and to give them such facts as he felt to be of interest regarding the country and its people. He had no ambition to be known in London as the author of the latest book on America.

As much cannot be affirmed of most English visitors to the United States in this period, whose writings we possess. For, as Dr. Thwaites has well said, "Every English traveler hither, whether his journey was that of a serious investigator or merely of a tourist eager to behold strange lands and new conditions, felt impelled to give his personal impressions in volumes of varying merit, evincing every shade of admiration and dislike." Many of these books were mere collections of letters or diaries; only a very small number were in the nature of systematic treatises. This was inevitable; but the unfortunate thing, from the standpoint of the historical student at least, is that most of these publications were composed with a definite purpose either to promote or to discourage emigration. In the one case, America was pictured in the most extravagant manner as a land possessing every desirable physical resource and condition, inhabited by a people of rare enlightenment, and offering to every newcomer all the delights of material prosperity, free institutions, and opportunity for unlimited advancement; in the other, the country was represented to be an unhealthy wilderness, defying the substantial advance of civilization, and the people to be the off-scourings of Europe, now retrograded almost to the level of savages.

Fordham represents the type of English emigrant, all too rare, who appreciated to the full the manifold inconveniences and deprivations of life in a new country but yet had the faith to believe that

the difficulties were only temporary and that incessant industry was all that was needed to transform
the crude backwoods settlements into flourishing
and enlightened commonwealths. Like other travelers, he saw many things — slavery, intemperance,
ignorance, lack of manners — of which he could not
but heartily disapprove, but he did not allow these
to blind him to the fundamental facts of American
opportunity and achievement. Without in any sense
posing as a seer, he was able to forecast with remarkable success the main lines along which the development of the country took place during the two
formative decades after he wrote. A sane optimism,
a clear insight, an honest purpose — these were the
young engineer's best qualifications as a portrayer
of conditions and a chronicler of events in the Middle West of his day.

F. A. O.

FORDHAM'S PERSONAL NARRATIVE
1817-1818

ORIGINAL PREFACE

THE following pages contain extracts from letters written by a young man to his friends in England. They were composed under every disadvantage: sometimes when the writer was surrounded by the noisy inhabitants of a smoky cabin, in his blanket tent, or in the bar room or no less public dormitory of a tavern. As he wrote to intimate and dear friends, and without any thought of their being presented to the world, the writer requests it may be remembered that what was meant for the eye of friendship alone is not a fair subject of criticism.

The author is now engaged in exploring the State of Illinois, and, probably will have further and better opportunities of describing this interesting country. Whether he will appear again before the public will be determined by the degree of favor now shown to him.

Nov. 2, 1818.

FORDHAM'S PERSONAL NARRATIVE

I

On board the Schooner George Whythe
Chesapeak Bay May 18th 1817.

OUR voyage was remarkably quick and, to those who were in health, agreeable.[1] We were only 30 days from Land to Land and 32 from the Downs to Cape Henry, the entrance to the Chesapeak. In the Gulf Stream we had stormy weather, but I think it rather added to the spirits of the party, than otherwise, for it afforded continual subject for conversation and admiration. I suppose you know that the Gulf Stream is a current of water which flows from the Gulf of Mexico round the point of Florida, up the coast of the United States; then spreading and turning gradually to the westward; less perceptibly as it leaves the coast, deposits the mud of the West Indies on the banks of Newfoundland, then passes Eastward; and ultimately, flowing Southward down the coast of Africa, is again carried by the trade winds into the Gulf of Mexico.

---

[1]The "America" (Captain Heth), on which Fordham took passage, sailed from Gravesend, March 30, 1817, bound for Richmond, Virginia. For a fuller account of the voyage than that here given see Morris Birkbeck, *Notes* (London, 1817), pp. 5-11. Some other interesting journals of voyages of Englishmen across the Atlantic in this period are: John Woods, *Two Years' Residence* (EARLY WESTERN TRAVELS, x, pp. 179-184); Adlard Welby, *Visit to North America* (EARLY WESTERN TRAVELS, xii, pp. 151-163); and William Faux, *Memorable Days* (EARLY WESTERN TRAVELS, xi, pp. 33-53).

It becomes so feeble and indistinct after it reaches the Azores that it loses its name. But westward of the Banks it runs at one or two miles per hour or even faster. Bad weather is always expected within its current which varies from 200 to 60 miles in width. If fear was felt at any time, no person in the cabin expressed it, and I believe none felt it. Indeed, a gale of wind comes on so gradually that it is not nearly so formidable as one would suppose it would be to a landsman. The wind rises — studding sails are taken in — the waves roughen — top gallant sails are struck, and top-sails are reefed — the sky looks dark and darker yet — the waves climb the ship's sides and the spray rattles against the cabin windows — the dead lights or shutters are put in — the Captain and the officers are looking out to windward — a squall is seen in the distance, upturning the billows and covering their crests with foam; — "Brail up the Mizen quick; bear up the helm a weather;"—it comes — we are prepared;—the vessel stoops before it, *snorts* through the waves, rises again and bounds onward like a stag. One day while we were at dinner M^r. B. observed that the ship *snorted* more than usual, when the first mate came in and said "Captain, a heavy squall is coming." The Captain left his knife and fork sticking in the ham he was carving, and went out to give the necessary orders. The ladies at the cabin door, the gentlemen wrapped in boat cloaks and holding by the shrouds, awaited its coming. It did come — the waves dashed over us — the leeward ports sunk deep

into the water; "Man the yards"—but, before a
man had reached a shroud, in one instant, the fore-
sail was split, rent from its yard, and carried in
tatters over the ship's side. After this we lay under stormstay sails for 24 hours, but the heavy swell
that followed the gale sprung the bowsprit and
foretopmast.

We all liked our Captain exceedingly; next to the
safety of the ship and the interest of the owners, the
comforts of his passengers was the object of his
attention. M^r. B. drew up a letter of thanks for his
kindness to us, which we all signed, and presented
to him the day before we left the ship; he was so
affected by it that he could not restrain his tears.

We cast anchor in Hampton Roads on Saturday
night,[1] and the next morning proceeded up James
River with a fair wind and a clear sky. The banks
of this noble stream are beautiful, but not very
healthy. Land is worth from 10 to 16 $ per acre.
After running up 90 miles in about 10 hours, we arrived at a mud-bank, called Harrison's Bar. A
consultation took place between the Captain and
Pilot about crossing it; at high tide it was filled
with about 12 feet of water; our ship drew about
15. After searching for the softest places, the ship
was steered into it with all sails set; but the wind
at that moment died away and of course we all got
stuck fast.[2]

---

[1] May 2, 1817.

[2] "May 6. Harrison's Bar.—This is a shoal of mud, which greatly
impedes the navigation, and in which we must be contented to lie
until the next tide, and we may easily content ourselves, as it is

The next morning the Jolly boat was sent ashore with part of the passengers, and the pinnace, decorated and manned with eight of the smartest sailors, took M^r. B., the ladies, and the Captain to M^r. H——'s, who is an acquaintance of the Captain's. M^r. H. was not at home, but M^{rs}. H. received the party with politeness. There was a great deal of company there and everything in and about the house was most elegant. After staying some time, sweetmeats were handed round by a train of black servants and the party received pressing invitations to return the next day.

I landed with the boys and young men on the opposite shore, on a most beautiful and picturesque bank which was covered with acacias in full blossom, almond trees covered with flowers of snowy whiteness, cedars, weeping willows, mountain ashes, laurestinas,[1] wild grape-vines, and almost every Shrub that is to be seen in the Green house or Pleasure grounds of an English gentleman. After penetrating this thicket, which edged the winding bank for many a mile, we found ourselves among fields of wheat and Indian corn, just springing out of the ground. The landscape was composed of dark forests crowning every hill, the sides partially cleared

---

a bend of the river, which is surrounded by all that is beautiful in woodland scenery, in the gayest dress of spring. We are fixed about the middle of the stream, which is four miles wide. Several rich plantations and substantial dwellings are in view."—Morris Birkbeck, *Notes*, p. 14. In more recent times Harrison's Bar has been known as Harrison's Landing. It is about twenty miles up the James from the mouth of the Chickahominy.

[1] The laurestina (*Viburnum tinus*) is an evergreen shrub which blooms during the winter months. It is a native of southern Europe.

and cultivated, and narrow vallies or rather ravines, clothed with shrubs which were beautiful beyond description scented the air with delightful perfumes, conducted streams of fresh water which were oftener heard than seen in the dark recesses of the thickets. Here, while a fervid sun rendered walking in the open fields painful, we enjoyed the most refreshing coolness, and birds of most beautiful plumage or of sweetest notes seemed to invite us to stay. The Mocking-bird which is here, as the Robin is in England, esteemed sacred, would scarcely avoid us, and partridges, turtle-doves, and hares started up at every step.

These delightful regions are cultivated by lazy Slaves, who are fat and comfortable enough in their general appearance, but who are never trusted out of the sight of the Overseers; nor are they, I am told, trustworthy.

After two days of excessive exertion, our ship was dragged through 300 yards of mud, into which she had sunk 3 feet. A few hours carried us to City point,[1] a poor village, situated on a beautiful, but unhealthy, spot. From City point the gentlemen went in gigs to Petersburg, about 12 miles off, to get Cleared of the Custom house. These

---

[1] City Point is located at the mouth of the Appomattox, about thirty miles below Richmond and ten northeast of Petersburg. It has never grown to be a place of importance.

[2] Petersburg is situated on the Appomattox River, about twenty-two miles south of Richmond. Its site, as well as that of Richmond, was selected by Colonel William Byrd, one of the most eminent Virginians of the early eighteenth century. The town was incorporated by the legislature of Virginia in 1748. During the closing campaigns of the Revolution, Petersburg was brought into

gigs were not quite equal to English ones. Having
been for some time an invalid, I was afraid of being
jolted, and tried to get a saddle-horse; but that was
not to be obtained. The saddle hurt the horse — or,
I should hurt the horse — or, ride too fast; — at last
a light sulky was found for me, which, when the
horse trotted, shook my poor bones unmercifully.
Our road was through forests of pine, live oak,
acacias, and many ornamental trees. Spaces of
cleared land occurred at intervals, with shabby farm
houses, and now and then fields worn out, and abandoned to the growth of young pines and weeds. The
land is not very good here, but the scenery beautiful.

Petersburg, a port and market town, was half
destroyed by fire two years ago. The old part consists of wooden houses, surrounded by balconies and
supported by posts. The Shops are like wooden
booths. The new part, which already contains 300
handsome brick houses, would shame most of the
country towns of England. After finishing our
business, we went to dine at a tavern with about 60

---

prominence by being captured by the British from Baron Steuben
in 1781, and by serving as an important stopping-point of Cornwal-
lis in the movement which culminated at Yorktown. When the Birk-
beck-Fordham party visited the place in 1817 to attest to the con-
tents of their baggage they found it the most flourishing in that
section of the state. "Petersburg," writes Birkbeck (*Notes,* pp.
15-16), "is growing into a place of importance, being the emporium
of export and import to a large district. Tobacco is the staple produce; and every article of British or German manufacture, the return. It is not quite two years since half the town was destroyed
by a fire, occasioned by some negroes playing at cards in a stable,
and it is already nearly rebuilt in the most substantial manner.
Two hundred capital brick houses were built last year. This vigorous revival under a calamity so general is a strong proof of general
prosperity."

farmers, who had just arrived from the race-ground. A violent rain detained the whole party all night, which gave us an opportunity of gaining some information from the most intelligent and communicative guests of the tavern. When I speak of a Virginian farmer, at least, such as I have hitherto seen, you must not imagine him to be a plainly dressed, clownish man: nothing is more unlike; he is usually a tall, pale, genteel looking man; his language is correct and good with no vulgarisms in pronunciation. He has a free, independent, look. His easy manners and loose long dress remind you of a Frenchman, only that the latter has most frequently something of a military appearance, which the Virginian has not. Their manners are too familiar, though not coarse. They used to be great duellists; but since the laws against duelling are enforced with rigour, the young men, I am told, carry dirks and decide their quarrels upon the spot. This, I am assured, is a common practice. One young man was cut in the hand by a dirk at the tavern we slept at, soon after we went to bed.[1]

M^r. B., having decided to go to the Ohio State as soon as he could, enquiries were made as to the most eligible mode of travelling. Indian corn being

---

[1] Birkbeck (*Notes*, p. 16), recounting the impressions gained during this enforced sojourn at the Petersburg tavern, writes: "A Virginian planter is a republican in politics, and exhibits the high-spirited independence of that character. But he is a slave-master, irascible, and too often lax in morals. A dirk is said to be a common appendage to the dress of a planter in this part of Virginia. I never saw in England an assemblage of countrymen who would *average* so well as to dress and manners: none of them reached anything like style; and very few descended to the shabby."

4

two $ per bushel at Richmond, and as in the Mountains it cannot be procured for any number of horses, I agreed to go down the River to Norfolk[1] in the first vessel that would take the heavy luggage. M[r]. B. and the rest of the party went to Richmond last Friday week in the Steam boat;[2]—then with the Phaeton and a light Jersey waggon they will proceed across the mountains westward.[3] On Satur-

---

[1] The next day (May 3) after the "America" anchored at Hampton Roads, Captain Heth went in the pilot-boat to Norfolk, fourteen miles distant, to make entry of the ship at the Custom House. He was accompanied by Birkbeck, who recorded in his *Notes* (p. 12) that the town had not fewer than ten thousand inhabitants and that "the streets are in right lines, sufficiently spacious, with wide paved causeways before the houses, which are good-looking and cleanly."

[2] This was May 9. In Birkbeck's *Notes* (pp. 19-20) there is an interesting description of the Virginia capital, in part as follows: "Richmond contains 13,000 inhabitants, nearly half of which are negroes. The hill, on which stands the Capitol, a building of commanding aspect, is inhabited by the more opulent merchants, and professional men, who have their offices in the lower town. Their houses are handsome, and elegantly furnished, and their establishments and style of living display much of the refinement of polished society. The town is generally well built, and increasing rapidly, whilst but little provision seems to be made in the country round for the accommodation of its inhabitants. The market is badly supplied; the common necessaries of life are excessively dear, and, excepting the article of bread, of bad quality. . . . It is worse supplied and at a dearer rate than any other place of equal size in the United States, or perhaps in the world. The town is forced up by the stimulus of commerce, whilst the surrounding country is groaning under the torpid influence of slavery: the cultivators are said to be jealous of its rising prosperity, instead of availing themselves, as they might, of the advantages it would afford as a market for their produce. . . . The enterprizing people are mostly strangers: Scotch, Irish, and especially New England men, or Yankees, as they are called, who fill every house as soon as it is finished."

[3] Birkbeck and his nine companions left Richmond May 17, "in two hacks, which are light coaches with two horses, and a Jersey waggon and one horse for the baggage." (*Notes*, p. 26.) Their route to the West was as follows: from Richmond by way of Fredericksburg to the Potomac River; thence to Washington by steamboat; thence by way of Fredericktown, Maryland, to McConnellstown [present McConnellsburg] Pennsylvania; thence along the

day I hailed a Schooner, bound to Norfolk, and agreed with the master, a free Negro, to take me for 30$. His miserable cabin contained Sailors, negroes, and a half-bre[e]d indian woman and her child.

At Norfolk I arrived on Monday morning. That day and the next I was employed in looking out and bargaining for a vessel to take me to Baltimore. I got an introduction to an English merchant residing at Norfolk, who gave me much assistance. I engaged a small bark to take the goods and myself for 44$, and sailed on Tuesday evening. On board this bark I am at this moment. It is a tight little Schooner, commanded by a respectable young man, only 22 years old, but he is married and has a family. His crew consists of two boys and one man younger than myself. Young as we all are I can assure you we are very careful: in fact, M^r. Dennis is rather too much so for my patience; for I want to get round to Cincinnati in time to join M^r. B. who wishes me to go with him in his exploring journey.

I have now been six days out from Norfolk and am yet 200 miles from Baltimore. The Schooner though nearly full of our luggage, is yet so lightly loaded, that she does not stand well against head winds when they blow hard. We have run into har-

Pennsylvania State Road to Pittsburg; thence on horseback through Ohio to Cincinnati, by way of Canonsburg and Washington (Pennsylvania) Wheeling (Virginia), and St. Clairsville, Zanesville, Somerset, Rushville, Lancaster, Chillicothe, Piketown, Greenfield, Leesburg, and Lebanon (Ohio); from Cincinnati to the English Prairie, in Edwards County, Illinois, by way of Madison, Lexington, Vincennes, Princeton, Harmony, and Mt. Vernon (Indiana), and Shawneetown, Illinois.

bour three times since we left Norfolk. The coasts of the Chesapeak thus far are low. The farm houses, which I have yet seen, are mean: the people live in a plain way. Even in Norfolk, though there is some splendor, there is little Comfort — English Comfort I mean. An air of lazy luxury pervades everything.

From Baltimore I shall proceed over land to Pittsburg. I must hire waggons for the luggage, and, if I am well enough, I shall walk with them. But, if I feel too weak for that, I shall go by the stages to Pittsburg, and thence down the Ohio to Cincinnati. My tour will be eleven or twelve hundred miles.[1]

---

[1] The routes to the West from Baltimore and Philadelphia, as well as the difficulties of the journey thither, were very well understood in England by reason of the numerous letters and pamphlets published by English travellers and settlers who had been over the ground. In 1817, for example, appeared John Bradbury's *Travels in the Interior of America in the Years 1809, 1810, and 1811*, in which the course to be pursued by the newly arrived emigrant was outlined as follows: "It shall be supposed that the design of the emigrant is to proceed to the countries east of the Alleghanies, therefore he ought not to stay more than two or three days in the city, which he can leave when he pleases, as great numbers of waggons start from Philadelphia to Pittsburg, or from Baltimore to Pittsburg or Wheeling, every day. The charge is by the hundred weight, both for passengers and their luggage, and the rate varies from five to seven dollars per hundred; but the men may go cheaper if they chuse to walk over the mountains, which is recommended. The waggoners travel with great economy: many of them carry a small camp-kettle with them to cook their provisions, and some have even a bed in their waggons, in which they sleep at night. A traveller who chooses to adopt a similar mode, may travel very cheap; or, as there are plenty of inns on the roads, he can be accommodated every night with beds, at a very reasonable rate. When the emigrant arrives at Pittsburg or Wheeling, he will find that numbers of Europeans and Americans are arriving there every day, and the same causes that operated against them in the maritime cities, as respects employment, will, in some degree, have an effect here; but as he will have occasion for information, it would be advisable for him to stop a few days to make enquiries. If we find

P. S. There is expected to be a great scarcity
of wheat. Flour at Norfolk is worth 14½$ per bar-
rel. Indian Corn, which is the food for the horses
and blacks, and much eaten by poor people, is 2$
per bushel. Corn bread, when new, is very pal-
atable, and, I believe, wholesome. I have eaten
scarcely any other.

When you consider I have been much engaged,
and that I am not quite in health, you will excuse
the negligent, loose, way, in which I have written
this letter. I have been afflicted with headaches ever
since the Seasickness left me, but I hope I shall re-
gain my strength, as I live very temperately. The
evening air is dangerous to new comers; for after a
hot day, the dew falls like rain. I have a fire lighted
in our little Cabin every evening. Wood costs nothing but the fetching. I have just been busying
myself in chopping up a fine deal board, which the

---

it necessary to descend the Ohio, the best mode of proceeding will
be to enquire for one or more families, who have intentions of going to the same neighbourhood as himself, who may join him in
the purchase of an *ark*, one of the kind of vessels in which families descend. These arks are built for sale, for the accommodation of families descending the river, and for the conveyance of
produce. They are flat-bottomed, and square at the ends, and are
all made of the same dimensions, being fifty feet in length, and
fourteen in breadth; which last is limited, because it often happens
that they must pass over the falls at Louisville, when the river is
at a low state, at which time they pass betwixt two rocks in the
Indian schute, only fifteen feet asunder. These arks are covered,
and are managed by a steering oar, which can be lifted out of the
water. The usual price is seventy-five dollars for each, which will
accommodate three or four families, as they carry from twenty-
five to thirty tons : and it frequently happens that the ark can be
sold for nearly what it cost, six or eight hundred miles lower down
the river." EARLY WESTERN TRAVELS, v, pp. 300-302. For other descriptions of Ohio River craft see p. 79, note.

boys found on the shore. It went against my conscience to burn such a piece of wood, which had scarcely a knot in it and would have made four or five steps for a handsome Staircase.

II

Character of the Virginians — Unhealthful physical conditions —
Baltimore — Communications between Baltimore and Pittsburg
— The Marylanders — The Pennsylvanians — The East and
West as fields for settlement.

Bedford,[1] in Bedford County
Pennsylvania, June 7th, 1817.

I THINK I gave you an account of my voyage up
the Chesapeak. That little trip made me more of a
Sailor than my passage across the Atlantic; and
I felt much more anxiety, as I had the charge of
goods worth at least a thousand pounds, which could
not be replaced. The whole crew of the little
Schooner were one night so fatigued that they fell

---

[1] The site of Bedford near the headwaters of the Juniata, was
first occupied in 1751, though the place was known for some time
as Raystown, from the name of its earliest settler. During his
campaign against Fort Duquesne in 1758, General Forbes selected
it as a location for a new fort, known as Fort Bedford, which in
the Indian wars that followed became a stronghold second in importance only to Fort Pitt in the contested territory of western
Pennsylvania. The town of Bedford was incorporated by the Pennsylvania legislature in 1766. By the end of the century it had come
to be important as the chief halting place for travellers and emigrants going westward over the wagon roads from either Philadelphia or Baltimore to Pittsburg. Practically every foreigner who
visited the West and left a record of his experiences and observations had something to say about the inevitable sojourn at Bedford.
Among such accounts of the place may be mentioned François
André Michaux, *Travels* (EARLY WESTERN TRAVELS, iii, p. 145);
Fortescue Cuming, *Sketches* (EARLY WESTERN TRAVELS, iv, pp. 63-
65); John Melish, *Travels*, ii, pp. 36-37; and Thomas Nuttall, *Journal* (EARLY WESTERN TRAVELS, xiii, pp. 39-41). Cuming, in 1807,
speaks in high terms of both the appearance of the town and the
manners of its people. He says it then contained about eighty
houses, with a school and a church. Melish, in 1811, says the
town was thriving and that it had 547 inhabitants. Visitors to the
town were generally struck with the beauty and healthfulness of
its location. On the development of this portion of Pennsylvania
Jones, *History of the Juniata Valley* (Philadelphia, 1856) may be
consulted to advantage.

asleep repeatedly while the vessel's head was plunging under every wave. I steered her four hours myself.

Of the Virginians I can say but little of my own observations, but I hear from all quarters that they are urbane, hospitable and generous. They have very little commercial enterprise; they live much on their own Plantations, which they cultivate with little spirit. Almost all of them deplore the existence of Slavery; though they think it must be continued, now it is introduced. They were fond of gaming and they were till lately great duellists, but both practices are partially put a stop to by Laws lately enacted. It seems there is something in the influence of the fervid sun, under which they live, or probably in their education; for now duelling is prevented, they do not quarrel the less frequently; but they (that is the young men) draw the dirks, which they usually wear, and stab one another upon very slight provocations.

It is said they are peculiarly addicted to Swearing: I do not think they are more so than the Marylanders and Pennsylvanians; but all Swear a great deal. They are a tall, elegantly shaped race of men. The gentlemen are fairer than Englishmen, their faces being always shaded by hats with extraordinarily broad brims. The poorer people and overseers are very swarthy: on the hills of the westward, very healthy, but on the low shores of the Chesapeak very much otherwise.

I landed very often; and, sometimes rambled for miles through the Pine woods with my gun. At every opening where I saw a house I used to make up to it, and always received an invitation to enter, and sometimes to share a meal.

The Ague and Fever are very common here. I gave away in these visits all my bark and laudanum. They would send a negro five miles through the woods, and as far with a canoe on the water, for one or two doses. In return they always sent milk or anything I wanted. The medical men in these districts have not much reputation. I have no doubt that, with an Edinburgh Dispensary, I could gain a good income in any of these unhealthy districts, if my conscience would allow me. The Eastern shores of the Chesapeak are lower, if possible, than the western, and more intersected with marshes, which emit a most offensive effluvia. Such is the quantity of decaying vegetable and animal substances on these Shores that the stench arises through the salt-water when touched by the keel of a boat. There are some rich meadows here, which cattle can scarcely keep down, however numerous they may be.

From Annapolis,[1] a beautiful little town seen

---

[1] The name Annapolis was given, in 1691, to the Protestant stronghold in Maryland which had formerly been known as Providence. This was at the time when Maryland became a royal province and the capital was taken away from the Catholic centre St. Mary's. The town was located on the Severn River, about two miles from its entrance to Chesapeake Bay. It grew very slowly and was a place of little consequence well down into the nineteenth century. There is a description of it as it was in 1807 in Melish, *Travels*, i, pp. 189-190.

from the water, to the Petapsco[1] the country is hilly and fine; thence to Baltimore is hilly, but bare of trees.

Baltimore,[2] except that it has not such Palaces as Paris can boast of, nor Churches like St. Paul's in London, nor is quite so picturesque as Rouen nor so grand in itself or in situation, is the most beautiful town I have ever seen. It has no bad streets; but all the liveliness, with scarcely any of the dirt, of a seaport. It contains 60,000 inhabitants. I lodged at the Fountain Inn, where at the time M^r. Munro, the president, has taken up his abode.

Do you ask me how I like this Country? Upon the whole very much. But there are many things to disgust an Englishman. There is too much Luxury; too much slavery in Virginia and Maryland. But, on the other hand, the country is beautiful, most of the people are well informed; some men among the higher orders are very gentlemanly, elegant in their manners and cultivated in their understandings.

I had several letters of introduction; and the gentlemen with whom I became acquainted gave me

[1] The Petapsco is a small stream flowing into Chesapeake Bay about twenty miles north of Annapolis and a short distance south of Baltimore.

[2] For a description of Baltimore in 1806-07 see Melish, *Travels*, i, pp. 184-185; in 1817, Fearon, *Sketches*, pp. 342-345; and in 1820, Woods, *Two Years' Residence* (EARLY WESTERN TRAVELS, x, pp. 187-196). Fearon's account is particularly interesting. He gives 60,-000 as an estimate of the population of the city.

much good advice respecting my journey and treated me with great kindness.

M^r. A. joined me at Baltimore.

The distance from this place to Pittsburg is 240 miles, across four ridges of mountains. The mail is six days going this distance — the waggons sixteen. They travel at 12, 15 or 20 miles per day. They avoid, as much as possible, the turnpike roads, & scramble over hills and mountains, where English waggons would be dashed to pieces; but these light carriages, built in a masterly way, & of the best materials, seem to be indestructible. The waggoners requested that we keep with them on the mountains; for the combined strength of several men is necessary to keep the waggons from upsetting in descending the cliffs. The horses would in England be admirably adapted for the gig or coach.[1]

Maryland, which I have now traversed from Baltimore to its Eastern extremity, is very hilly; and westward, very mountainous. Even the plains between the ranges would be reckoned hilly in England. They are in general very rich; and, where this

---

[1] In the earlier part of the great era of westward migration the most important thoroughfare from the New England and Middle states to the Ohio Valley was the Pennsylvania Road, or "Pittsburg Pike," built in 1785-87 by act of the Pennsylvania legislature. It extended 197 miles from Carlisle to Pittsburg, along very nearly the same route as the present highway between the two places. Even after the construction of the Cumberland Road, in 1806-1818, from Cumberland, Maryland, to Wheeling, Virginia (and subsequently as far westward as Vandalia, Illinois), the majority of traders and travellers from Baltimore and Washington, as well as from more northern points, made use of this route, coming into it generally from the south at McConnellstown (present McConnellsburg), 130 miles from Pittsburg. Travellers during the period following the War of 1812 were invariably astonished not only at the

is the case, the people are so too. A great many
Quakers among the Marylanders are Slave-holders.
They are not like the Virginians; being a mixture
of Dutch, German, Irish; boorish when poor, rather
reserved when rich; very inquisitive, but soon re-
pulsed. I have been but 15 or 16 days among them,
so you must take my observations as giving only a
hasty sketch.

As soon as I entered Pennsylvania, I remarked a
different people. Here are no slaves; white people
are seen working in the fields and roads. They are
cleaner than the Dutch, but the latter are not always
boorish. If Maryland be the land of hills, Pennsylvania is the land of mountains. We have struggled
over four distinct ridges — the North Mountains —
the South Mountains — the Cove Mountains & the
Sidelong Hills. The two last are infested with ban-
ditti, after whom about 40 young men went with
their rifles about a week since. These men have
not yet attacked travellers, but they plunder farmers

---

difficulties with which the waggoners had to contend on their trips
along this wilderness highway, but also at the amount of traffic
actually carried on under such disadvantages. Writing at Bedford in October, 1818, Thomas Nuttall says, in his *Journal*: "To
judge of the inland commerce carried on betwixt Philadelphia and
Pittsburg, a stranger has but to view this road at the present season. All day I have been brushing past waggons heavily loaded
with merchandise, each drawn by five and six horses; the whole
road in fact appears like the cavalcade of a continued fair" (EARLY
WESTERN TRAVELS, xiii, p. 41). Birkbeck (*Notes*, p. 36), writing in
May, 1817, says that the money paid annually for the conveyance of
goods on the road from Philadelphia to Pittsburg exceeded £300,000
sterling. For contemporary descriptions of the traffic westward over
the Pennsylvania highways see Cuming, *Sketches* (EARLY WESTERN
TRAVELS, iv, pp. 25-76); Melish, *Travels*, ii, pp. 24-54; Fearon,
Sketches, pp. 183-189; and Woods, *Two Years' Residence* (EARLY
WESTERN TRAVELS, x, pp. 197-216).

of their clothes and cattle. They have women with them, and live in wigwams among the rocks.

My health having suffered from a severe cold, which I could not attend to while I was travelling with the waggons and as I could hear nothing of the three hindermost, I stopped here yesterday at noon. M^r. A. went on with the first; to-day the last came up. I shall proceed to-morrow by the Stage to the foot of the Allegany mountains; and if I hear that the roads over them are bad, I shall again march with the foremost waggon which contains the Piano. We have already saved it from being dashed to pieces twice: it is a high load, as the case would not lie at the bottom of the waggon. If I hear a good account of the road I shall go on in the Stage to Pittsburg, which I shall then reach in three days. At Pittsburg I hope to meet the ladies: M^r. B. and ———— I suppose are gone to explore the South Western country.

I have visited to-day the mineral springs; about a mile and a quarter from this little town.[1] I met there two Philadelphians, amiable young men. It was quite refreshing to converse with people of refined and English manners, after having lived with waggoners ten days. They tell me that land within 20 miles of Philadelphia is worth 50$ 100$ 150$

---

[1] In writing of his visit to Bedford in 1807 Cuming (*Sketches*) says that some chalybeate springs strongly impregnated with sulphur had lately been discovered in the neighborhood of the town, to which great medicinal virtues were attributed. (EARLY WESTERN TRAVELS, iv, p. 65). Melish (*Travels*, ii, p. 37), in 1811, remarks that the Bedford springs had by that time become a notable watering place and that he found there "a vast concourse of people collected from different places, some of them very distant."

p^r. acre. Then it is one's own; few taxes, no tythes, good market, society, & European papers daily.

I am not sure that English elderly people would do right to pass the mountains. The ocean is a mere nothing; and if all I hear of Philadelphia and N. York be true, an English family with moderate property may fancy themselves in England *improved* on a hired farm. For young men, everybody agrees, that the Western territory will be the best to settle in. But, alas, it is another world; not only distant but distinct from Europe; more connected with the Spanish Main, with the East Indies even, than with England. The bright side of the prospect is, that the further West (I quote Gen. Wilkinson)[1] the more honest, the more generous the people are. The hunter of the Prairie, of St. Louis, or the woods of Illinois or Tennessee, will divide his venison with you; he will rather strip his shirt off his back than take a cent from you. These men retire from the never ceasing flow of population; with this comes a

[1] James Wilkinson was a Marylander who, after a rather dubious career in the Revolution, went to Kentucky to engage in business and repair his fortunes. In the decade of controversy between the people of the south-western United States and the Spaniards of Louisiana regarding the right of the former to the navigation of the Mississippi River, Wilkinson followed the demagogic plan of appearing to champion the interests of the Americans while at the same time acting as the paid agent of the Spaniards to bring about a revolt of the inhabitants of Kentucky and Tennessee and the dismemberment of the Union. Despite his intrigues, in 1796 he succeeded General Anthony Wayne as commander-in-chief of the United States army. In 1805 he was appointed governor of Louisiana. While holding this important office he first co-operated with Aaron Burr in his ambitious designs, then betrayed him. At the outbreak of the War of 1812 he was removed from his western post. After an inglorious part in the conduct of that war he retired, in 1815, to an extensive estate which he possessed near the City of Mexico, and there he died in 1825.

laborious, enterprising, set of men, mingled with sharpers, desperadoes, &c. Then rise towns and cities.

Give my kindest remembrances to all friends — I cannot mention all the names that I value. Excuse the incorrectness of this letter, for time is seldom at my command — you have a better or truer description of what I see and feel than a more laboured one would give.

III

Pittsburg June 17. 1817.

THOUGH I have so long delayed, yet I have not forgotten to write. Several times I have begun a letter, which I wanted time to finish. I have put it in my travelling trunk, seen more, and found that I had written down first impressions, which upon deeper insight I have discovered to be erronious.

Of this singular country nothing is known in England: the Inhabitants of its cities even do not know it, so various and contrasted are the materials of which its population is composed, so strange is the structure of society, so imperfectly is it cemented by opinion.

Of the Inhabitants of the Northern States, or Yankees, I have seen nothing: they have the reputation of being very keen, shrewd, enterprising and industrious. The Merchants of the Cities are like the Merchants of England: indeed, most of them finish their commercial education in England, France, or Holland.

But the inhabitants of the interior of Pennsylvania are very different. Coarse in their manners, inquisitive to a tormenting degree, careless of giving pain or offense, and obstinate in persisting in their rudeness: these are the most common features in their characters. They are chiefly of Dutch, Ger-

man, or Irish extraction; and in general seem to
have preserved all the vices of their forefathers, and
to have acquired a few others. Whisky is very cheap.
With the labour of an hour a man may purchase as
much as will make him ferocious, if not drunk; he
fights with the first drunkard he meets, and they
bite each other like dogs, or tear out each other's
eyes. Perhaps disgust has induced me to shade
the picture too darkly.[1] Disappointment too has
deepened my dislike of the Pennsylvanians. Yet
this is the country of *Penn* — whose capital is called
the City of Brotherly Love. Travelling across a
mountainous track, which will never be thickly inhabited, I have seen the worst of its population.
There are, however, bright exceptions — angels
among these Demons. I was taken ill at the house

---

[1]The testimony of travellers generally in the first quarter of the
nineteenth century tends to bear out Fordham in his estimate of the
western Pennsylvanians. François André Michaux tells in his
Travels of what he saw at Bedford in 1802 as follows: "The day of
our arrival was a day of rejoicing for the country people, who had
assembled together in this little town to celebrate the suppression
of the tax laid upon the whiskey distilleries; rather an arbitrary
tax, that had disaffected the inhabitants of the interior against the
late president, Mr. Adams. The public houses, inns, and more especially the one where we lodged, were filled with the lower class
of people, who made the most dreadful riot, and committed such
horrible excesses, that is almost impossible to form the least idea
of. The rooms, stairs, and yard were strewed with drunken men;
and those who had still the power of speech uttered nothing but
the accents of rage and fury. A passion for spirituous liquors is
one of the features that characterise the country people belonging
to the interior of the United States. This passion is so strong, that
they desert their homes every now and then to get drunk in public
houses; in fact. I do not conceive there are ten out of a hundred
who have resolution enough to desist from it a moment provided
they had it by them, notwithstanding their usual beverage in summer is nothing but water, or sour milk" (EARLY WESTERN TRAVELS,
iii, p. 144). The tax to which Michaux refers was the excise on
whiskey which had led to the Whiskey Rebellion of 1794 and which
had been repealed by Congress, much to the delight of the Pennsyl-

of a German in Bedford County—a tavern frequented by waggoners; if I had been a son, I could not have been better treated. The landlady prescribed for me and nursed me, the sons came to chat to me at my bedside, and the old man never passed my chamber door without enquiring how I was. Books were borrowed for me in the Town, and I read the Romances of M^{rs}. Radcliffe[1] amidst scenery scarcely less wild than the Vallies of the Appennines, or the shores of the Adriatic.

In Maryland, a slave state, the people are more mild and civilized. The Virginians, though dissipated, are gentlemen. I am told by a person of this town that I shall universally find a good society and polished manners in Slave States, and the reverse where slavery is not allowed. If this be the case, how superior is England to America, as a place of residence, to those who can afford to stay there!

vanians, in the spring of 1802. Cuming, writing at Bedford in January, 1807, says of the people of that vicinity: "So far do they carry this mania for whiskey that to procure it, they in the most niggardly manner deny themselves even the necessaries of life; and, as I was informed by my landlord Fleming, an observing and rational man, countrymen while attending the courts (for they are generally involved in litigation, of which they are very fond) occupy the bar rooms of the taverns in the country towns, for several days together, making one meal serve them each day, and sometimes two, and even three days — but drinking whiskey without bounds during the same time" (EARLY WESTERN TRAVELS, iv, pp. 62-63). Melish (*Travels*, ii, p. 51), in 1811, sought to explain, if not to disprove, the excessive use of spirituous liquors in the back country by showing that on the frontiers cider and malt liquors could not easily be had.

[1] Anne Radcliffe (1764-1823) was one of the most popular English writers of fiction in the first quarter of the nineteenth century. Among her numerous romances may be mentioned *The Castles of Athlin and Dunbayne: a Highland Story; The Italian: or The Confessional of the Black Penitents; The Mysteries of Udolpho; The Romance of the Forest;* and *A Sicilian Romance.* These stories, by their appeal to the love of the wonderful and the supernatural, marked a new departure in English novel-writing.

The Southern States, at least Georgia and the Carolinas, must be cultivated by blacks or abandoned. The heat there is so excessive in August that to walk a mile in the Sun would subject a European to the most imminent danger. The landed Proprietors of those States are hospitable and generous, but not so refined as the Virginians. They make great profits from their plantations; but they are usually in debt, & are dissipated and indolent.

The climate of the United States, from the Latitude of 39°North, is very severe. Sleighs are seen at every house. The Monongahela, which is rolling its turbid waves beneath my window, is frozen across every winter, and loaded waggons pass to the opposite bank; yet now the Thermometer I think would be as high as 90 in the shade. I could not venture out in the Sun without suffering for my imprudence, now I am in ill health. When I recover I shall be more hardy. When I crossed the Alleganies the leaves on the Trees were frost bitten on each side, and the weather here is as hot as it is ever known to be in England. . . .

The baggage amounts to 9,000 lbs. weight, contained in about 70 packages. I have sent off half of it under the care of M^r. A., in a keel boat. The remainder is not come in, and if it does not arrive tonight, I shall tomorrow take a horse and go in search of it. M^r. B.'s Phaeton was left in Virginia. The party travelled by the Stage as far as it was safe from M'cConnal's town[1] within 14 miles of this

[1]McConnellstown (the present McConnellsburg, in Fulton County,

place. They walked 120 miles across the Mountains, along roads of which you can have no idea. . . .

If the Ladies should be left at Cincinnati, I believe they will proceed with me by water to St. Louis, Missouri Territory.[1] Kentucky or the Missouri Territory, I am inclined to think, will be our choice. I have sent a line of route which I obtained from Gen. ——— which strongly recommends the Prairies of St. Louis. . . .

Pennsylvania), was the point at which the lines of travel from Baltimore and Washington toward Pittsburg merged with the Pennsylvania State Road. It is approximately one hundred miles from Baltimore and 130 miles from Pittsburg. Its site was first occupied by Fort Lyttleton, one of the chain of frontier posts built in 1756 for the protection of the western Pennsylvania border. Under date of June 17, 1803, Thaddeus M. Harris, a Massachusetts traveller, writes of the town, in his *Journal,* as follows: " Passing the Sideling Hills, we reach McConnel's town, a delightful, well-watered village in Bedford County, Pennsylvania, to dine. It is situated in the valley, or, as it is called "the Cove," between Sideling and North Mountains. It has been built eight years; contains about eighty houses, several of them handsomely built with brick or stone, a number of stores and shops, and a small Dutch meeting-house " (Early Western Travels, iii, p. 367). Melish (*Travels,* ii, pp. 34-35), in 1811, wrote that the place had eighty or ninety houses and about five hundred inhabitants. Fearon (*Sketches,* pp. 187-191) gives some interesting information about the place as he found it in October, 1817.

[1] St. Louis was founded in 1764 by Pierre Laclède Liguest and a company of followers, representing a French fur company. The town early gained a considerable population by reason of the fact that France had but recently yielded the territory east of the Mississippi to England and at least a third of the inhabitants of the ceded region at once withdrew to the new post on the western bank of the river. The town was incorporated in 1809 and in the following year the census showed that it had a population of 1,000. By 1818 it had 3,500 inhabitants, and by 1821, 5,600. On the history of St. Louis see Elihu H. Shepard, *The Early History of St. Louis and Missouri* (St. Louis, 1870); Frederic L. Billon, *Annals of St. Louis in its Early Days under the French and Spanish Dominations* (St. Louis, 1886); and Thomas Scharf, *History of Saint Louis City and County* (Philadelphia, 1883). Lewis C. Beck, *Gazetteer of the States of Illinois and Missouri* (Albany, 1823), pp. 324-331, has a good description of the city about 1822, with map.

Having said so much against the commonalty of this Republic, I ought to say, that from the gentlemen, and there *are* gentlemen here, I have met with kindness, politeness and hospitality. M * * N * *, DeG* * of N * * and some others, remind me of those I most love and esteem in England.

Excuse this bad writing; having just been bled, I cannot mend my pen, and the heat makes my head ache. I shall not close the letter, 'till I leave this place.

June 19th: Since writing the above, I have been in agreeable parties — a higher set. I have met with women, whose Manners are quite English, and whose personal appearance and attractions would be admired anywhere.

I am informed that M^r. B. has reached Cincinnati, and that he intends leaving the ladies there. I am going to embark on a flat boat; my provisions are already on board. Cincinnati is 500 miles hence, and I shall be 10 days on the voyage.

IV

Methods of earlier writers on the West — Pittsburg — Industries of the vicinity — Flat-boats and keels on the Ohio — The start down the river — Neville's Island — Logstown — Beavertown — Wheeling — Fish Creek — A thunder-storm — Marietta — The Muskingham [Muskingum] — Blennerhassett's Island — Galliopagus [Gallipolis] — Portsmouth — Manchester —Maysville — Augusta — Arrival at Cincinnati.

On the Ohio River June 22.

. . . If it be observed that my letters contain no information concerning the state of the country, you may say in my defence, that I have but little opportunity to make correct observations; I have something else to do. It is very easy to write letters and books, too, as Mellish, Wild[1] and others have done. They go to a Tavern-keeper, pump from

---

[1] No trace is obtainable of any work on Western history or topography by a writer of this name. In a letter to the Editor Dr. R. G. Thwaites has suggested that Fordham intends here to mention Isaac Weld, Jr., whose *Travels through the States of North America and the Provinces of Upper and Lower Canada in 1795-97* (London, 1799) was well known in both England and America. This seems the most plausible explanation of the doubtful reference.

John Melish, *Travels in the United States of America in the Years 1806 & 1807, and 1809, 1810 & 1811* (Philadelphia, 1812). Melish was a Scotchman who visited the United States for the first time in 1806, in the pursuit of commercial interests. During the next six years most of his time was spent in this country. He tells us that prior to his first visit he read all the "Travels in America" that he could lay hold of, but found them uniformly unsatisfactory — in some cases because of the ignorance and superficiality of the authors, in others because the facts had been twisted or obscured with a view to promoting or discouraging emigration. Hence he resolved to utilize his opportunities for observation in the preparation of a full and unprejudiced description of the country and the various elements of its population. His earlier travels took him through New England, the Middle States, and much of the South; and in 1810-11, as the relations of Great Britain and the United States became more strained he came to the conclusion that there would be no profit in international trade for some time to come, and that the lull could be best occupied by him with a tour through the West.

him all he chooses to tell them, and set it down: nine times in ten the information is very incorrect, sometimes purposely distorted. No dependence can be placed on any representation but that of an intelligent, honest man, long resident in the country, and who is personally well disposed toward you.

When I arrived at Pittsburg I went to M^r. B. of that place with letters of introduction. As I was very ill, I consulted M^{rs}. B. about having Medical advice. She recommended me to D^r. M. and to him I went;—he was a sensible clever man & set me up for 6\$. I expected to have paid 20\$.

Pittsburg[1] contains about 10,000 inhabitants,

Having carefully planned the places he desired to visit and the inquiries he desired to make as he went along, he set out from Baltimore June 3, 1811. It was late autumn before he returned to the East, and with him he carried a vast amount of information regarding Kentucky, Ohio, and other parts of the western country, which he proceeded to put in shape for publication. The result was the two volumes published the next year, embodying his observations on all sections of the United States — East, South, and West — which he had been able to visit. The value of Melish's writings is considerably greater than Fordham's remarks would lead one to suppose.

[1] In 1754, by command of Marquis Duquesne, governor of Canada, Fort Duquesne was built in the angle of the Monongahela and Allegheny rivers by a party of French under the leadership of M. de la Jonquier. The site selected for the fortification was exactly that of the later city of Pittsburg. For four years the French contrived to hold the place against the hostile English, but in November, 1758, when General Forbes undertook a well-planned campaign against it longer tenure seemed impossible and the fort was evacuated and burned by the commandant De Lignery. An English fort built forthwith somewhat further up the Monongahela received the name Fort Pitt, in honor of the Earl of Chatham; and by common consent the town which in time began to grow up around the stronghold was known as Pittsburg. The location of this town at the junction of the two leading rivers of western Pennsylvania and the beginning of the Ohio made it easily the most important gateway to the West. Some travellers, traders, and emigrants went westward by a route further to the north along the line of the lower Great Lakes, and others went by a southern route through the Cum-

mostly engaged in manufactures. The land around is fertile, though too hilly. It is pretty well cleared near the town, but 10 miles off the country is an immense forest, broken into and gapped by settlers. The farmers live well and work rather hard. Their servants are paid 75 cents per day and are boarded — in the morning with meat and coffee, hot meat and whisky at dinner and coffee, cold meat, and vegetables for Supper. Farming is not reckoned very

berland Gap; but travel from the entire eastern coast tended strongly to converge upon Pittsburg, where the Ohio became the great avenue for four or five hundred miles, in its lower course inviting settlers to spread out again toward both north and south. Practically all of the European elements that came into the West advanced thither from New York, Philadelphia, and Baltimore by way of Pittsburg. The result was that nearly every emigrant or traveller who wrote letters to friends at home, or published more pretentious accounts of the new country, had a good deal to say about Pittsburg. It may be of interest to cite a few of the most important of these early descriptions of the place, including some by American writers. François André Michaux (*Travels*), in 1802, says that the town had 400 houses and was growing rapidly. He points out how the place was losing its importance as a military post and acquiring significance of a new sort as a medium of commerce between the East and the West (EARLY WESTERN TRAVELS, iii, pp. 156-163). Cuming, on the occasion of his visit in February, 1807, got a less favorable impression — of the town itself, if not of its people. He found but a single paved street and was struck with the blackened appearance of all out-door objects, due to the already considerable use of coal. According to him (*Sketches*), in March, 1808, there were 17 streets, 236 brick houses, 361 wooden ones, 50 stores, 24 taverns, and several factories. He gives a very detailed classification of the population industrially, and a careful statement of the prices of all important commodities, concluding that "either as a trading or a manufacturing town, Pittsburg for situation, is not excelled in the United States, and it bids fair to become the emporium of the centre of the federal union" (EARLY WESTERN TRAVELS, iv, pp. 76-87, 242-255). Melish (*Travels*, ii, pp. 54-63), in 1811, says that the population of the town the previous year was 4,768 and prophesies that " it will become one of the largest towns in America and one of the greatest manufacturing cities in the world "— its manufactures being already valued at more than $1,000,000 annually. Thomas Hulme (*Journal*) says of the city in 1818: " This place surpasses even my expectations, both in natural resources and in extent of manufactures. Here are the materials for every species of manufacture, nearly, and of excellent quality and in profusion; and these

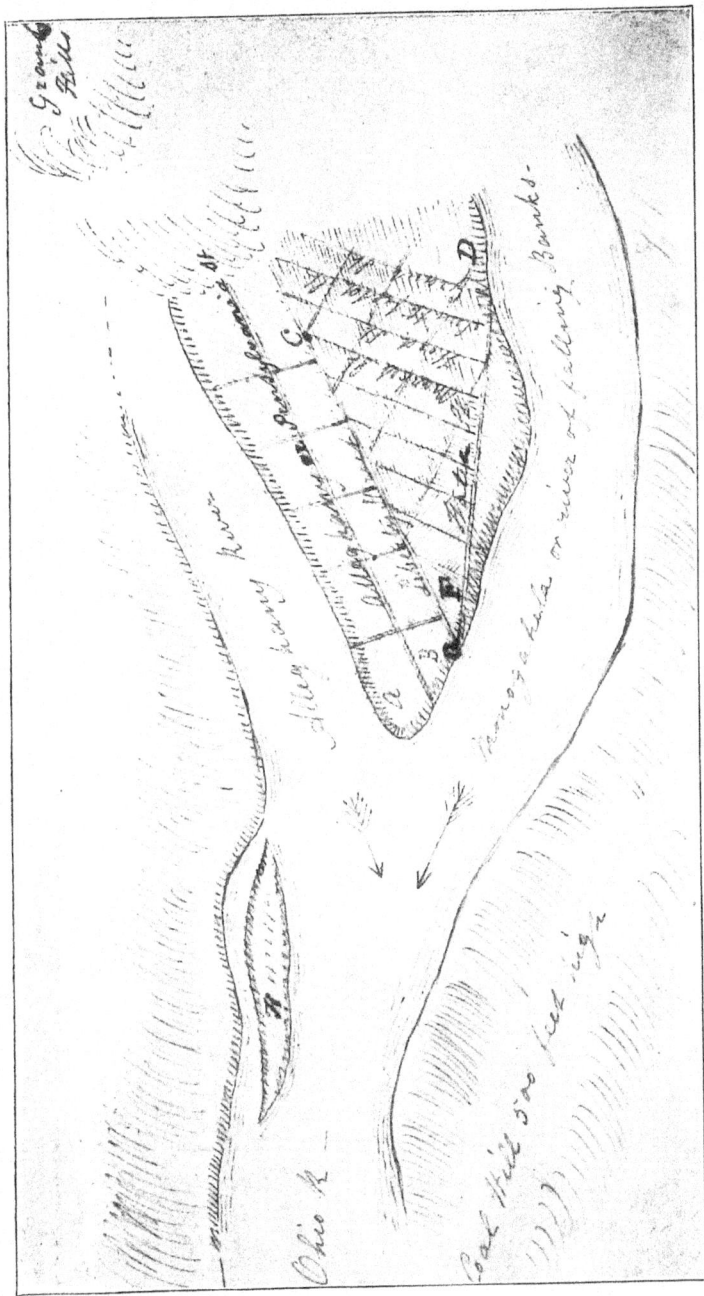

PLAN OF PITTSBURG IN 1817

A—Site of Fort Du Quesné   D—Bakewell's glass works
B—Fort Pitt   F—O'Hara's brewhouse
C—City hotel, where I lodged   G—Shipyard
H—Col. Killbuck's island, a chief of the six nations

profitable, but there are many able, that is rich, farmers. A Saw Mill is very profitable. One on a constant stream, costing 6 or 700$ will earn its value in one year; and sometimes a great deal more. When worked by steam and connected with a Grist Mill, it is an excellent business. It then requires a capital of 13 or 1400£ sterling. Tradesmen at Pittsburg live well and save money; but they complain of hard times, because Peace has thrown the Ocean trade into New Orleans, which they in War monopolized.[1]

M[r]. Bakewell's glass works are admirable: he has

means have been taken advantage of by skilful and industrious artisans and mechanics from all parts of the world. There is scarcely a denomination of manufacture or manual profession that is not carried on to a great extent, and, as far as I have been able to examine, in the best manner. The manufacture of iron in all the different branches, and the mills of all sorts, which I examined with the most attention, are admirable" (EARLY WESTERN TRAVELS, x, pp. 35-37). Other descriptions by writers of the period are: Morris Birkbeck, *Notes*, pp. 40-48; Fearon, *Sketches*, pp. 199-216; Estwick Evans, *Pedestrious Tour* (EARLY WESTERN TRAVELS, viii, pp. 247-255); James Flint, *Letters* (EARLY WESTERN TRAVELS, ix, pp. 82-89); John Woods, *Two Years' Residence* (EARLY WESTERN TRAVELS, x, pp. 217-218); Wm. Tell Harris, *Remarks*, pp. 89-90; Thomas Nuttall, *Journal* (EARLY WESTERN TRAVELS, xiii, pp. 44-45); and George W. Ogden, *Letters* (EARLY WESTERN TRAVELS, xix, pp. 26-28). An older popular history of Pittsburg is Neville B. Craig's *History of Pittsburg* (Pittsburg, 1851); a recent book on the subject is T. J. Chapman, *Old Pittsburg Days* (Pittsburg, 1900).

[1] Fearon in 1817, Estwick Evans in 1818, and Adlard Welby in 1819 agree that the trade of Pittsburg was, if not actually declining, at least not making appreciable growth. As a matter of fact, while the "hard times" of which Fordham speaks did not continue and the commerce of Pittsburg expanded remarkably during the next ten years, it was nevertheless true that the city had reached the critical point in its history where the carrying trade must give place to manufacturing as the staple industry and source of wealth; indeed the transition was already far progressed. The commercial relations of Pittsburg and New Orleans before and during the war are well described by François André Michaux as follows: "The major part of the merchants settled at Pittsburgh, or in the environs, are the partners, or else the factors, belonging to the houses at

excellent artists, both French and English. His Cut Glass equals the best I have seen in England.[1]

Brewing succeeds well here, especially the Porter Brewery. New Orleans is the principal market for it. The Pottery business must be very profitable; a plate, worth a 1^d. in England, sells here for 6^d. Distilling on a small scale answers well: many farmers are distillers.

I met some Baltimore acquaintances here, Messrs. E—— Senr. & Junr. The old man took me

Philadelphia. Their brokers at New Orleans sell, as much as they can, for ready money; or rather, take in exchange cottons, indigo, raw sugar, the produce of Low Louisiana, which they send off by sea to the houses at Philadelphia and Baltimore, and thus cover their first advances. The barge-men return thus by sea to Philadelphia or Baltimore, whence they go by land to Pittsburgh and the environs, where the major part of them generally reside. Although the passage from New Orleans to one of these two ports is twenty or thirty days, and that they have to take a route by land of three hundred miles to return to Pittsburgh, they prefer this way, being not so difficult as the return by land from New Orleans to Pittsburgh, this last distance being fourteen or fifteen hundred miles. . . . The navigation of the Ohio and Mississippi is so much improved of late that they can tell almost to a certainty the distance from Pittsburgh to New Orleans, which they compute to be two thousand one hundred miles. The barges in the spring season usually take forty or fifty days to make the passage, which two or three persons in a *pirogue* make in five and twenty days." *Travels* (EARLY WESTERN TRAVELS, iii, p. 159).

[1] The first glass factory west of the Alleghanies was built at Pittsburg by General James O'Hara in 1797. That of Bakewell, Pears and Company was established in 1808. Thomas Nuttall, who visited Pittsburg in 1818 on his way to the Arkansas Territory, writes: "The day after my arrival I went through the flint-glass works of Mr. Bakewell, and was surprised to see the beauty of this manufacture, in the interior of the United States, in which the expensive decorations of cutting and engraving (amidst every discouragement incident to a want of taste and wealth) were carried to such perfection. The productions of this manufacture find their way to New Orleans, and even to some of the islands of the West Indies. The president, Monroe, as a liberal encourager of domestic manufactures, had on his visit to those works given orders for a service of glass, which might indeed be exhibited as a superb specimen of this elegant art." *Journal* (EARLY WESTERN TRAVELS, xiii, p. 45).

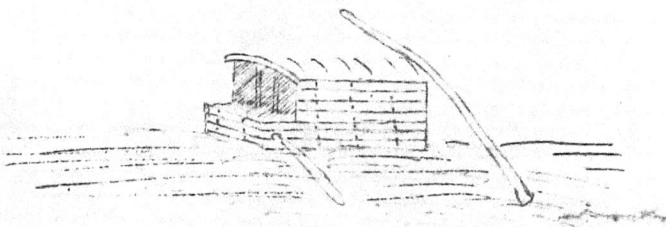

OHIO RIVER FLATBOAT (A), AND KEELBOAT (B)

to see his son's manufactory of Steam Engines and his Foundery. Seventy men were employed in the different works.

I sent off the first load of baggage under the care of M^r. A., and when the remainder arrived I hired freight on board a flat boat for 50 cents per cwt. These flat boats or Orleans boats as they are called in the Western Waters are from 12 to 25 feet wide, and from 30 to 90 feet long. They are sold when they arrive at their place of destination, and broken up. Not a 100 nails are used in building one, but they are stuck together with wooden pins. They will carry 700 barrels of flour. They cost 1$ p^r. foot in length and sell for ¼$. They are manned by four men each, and a pratoon. In the Mississippi double that number is necessary for the stream runs eight miles an hour: and is full of Eddies. Goods are brought up the river on keels or keelboats, which require 12 or 24 men to row and pole them against the current. It was in such a boat that Lewis and Clarke ascended the Missouri; it was built at Pittsburg.[1]

---

[1] The information here given regarding the various sorts of craft navigating the Ohio about 1817 may be supplemented by the following passage from Estwick Evans's *Pedestrious Tour,* published in 1819: "The boats which float upon the Ohio are various,— from the ship of several hundred tons burthen, to the mere skiff. Very few if any very large vessels, however, are now built at Pittsburgh, or indeed at any other place on the Ohio. They were formerly built on this river, particularly at Pittsburgh and Marietta; but the difficulties incident to getting them to the ocean, have rendered such undertakings unfrequent. An almost innumerable number of steam-boats, barks, keels, and arks, are yearly set afloat upon this river, and upon its tributary streams. The barks are generally about one hundred tons burthen, have two masts, and are rigged as schooners, and hermaphrodite brigs. The keels have, frequently, covered decks, and sometimes carry one

On Thursday, at noon, I went on board my Kentucky boat: there was another lashed to it. Having bid my friends farewell, we pushed off into the middle of the stream, which here runs at 3 miles an hour.[1] The bank of the river on our left was high, abrupt, and covered with trees. On our right it was hilly, but not precipitous. Col. Killbuck's island

mast. These and also the barks are sometimes rowed and sometimes moved up the river by poling, and by drawing them along shore with ropes. The flat-boat or ark is of a clumsy construction; but very burthensome. Its foundation consists of sills like those of a house, and to these is trunneled a floor of plank. The sides are of boards loosely put together, and the top is covered in the same way. The bottom of the boat, and so much of the sides as come in contact with the water, are caulked. Some of this kind of boats will carry four or five hundred barrels of flour, besides considerable quantities of bacon, cheese, and other produce. On the deck of, the ark are two large oars, moving on pivots, and at the stern there is a large steering oar. The progress of the ark is principally in floating with the current; and the oars are seldom used excepting for the purpose of rowing ashore. The business carried on by boats, on the Ohio and the Mississippi, is immense. The freight of goods up and down these rivers is high; and the freighting business here is exceedingly profitable. No property pays so great an interest as that of steamboats on these rivers. A trip of a few weeks yields one hundred per cent upon the capital employed. The arks, and, generally speaking, the keels, when they reach New Orleans, seldom return up the river again. The former are sold for lumber." (EARLY WESTERN TRAVELS, viii, pp. 256-257.) Another description of an Ohio River "ark" may be found in Thaddeus M. Harris's *Journal* (EARLY WESTERN TRAVELS, iii, p. 335). For the steamboat traffic on the Ohio and Mississippi see, p. 106, note. There is an interesting chapter on the evolution of river craft in Archer B. Hulbert *Waterways of Westward Expansion* (HISTORIC HIGHWAYS OF AMERICA, ix, pp. 100-150).

[1] Among other interesting narratives of the descent of the Ohio by travellers and emigrants of this period may be mentioned: François André Michaux, *Travels* (EARLY WESTERN TRAVELS, iii, p. 168, ff.); Fortescue Cuming, *Sketches* (EARLY WESTERN TRAVELS, iv, p. 87, ff.); John Melish, *Travels* (ii, p. 84, ff.); James Flint, *Letters from America* (EARLY WESTERN TRAVELS, ix, p. 89, ff.); Thomas Nuttall, *Journal* (EARLY WESTERN TRAVELS, xiii, p. 47, ff.); Thomas Hulme, *Journal* (EARLY WESTERN TRAVELS, x, p. 38, ff.); William Faux, *Memorable Days* (EARLY WESTERN TRAVELS, xi, p. 167, ff.); William Tell Harris, *Remarks*, pp. 90-99; and John Woods, *Two Years' Residence* (EARLY WESTERN TRAVELS, x, pp. 222-256.)

is well farmed by his tenants. This is not often the case: very little land is rented here.

Chartier's creek,[1] a pretty shaded stream, was the first break in the coal-hill on the left. A romantic wooden bridge spanned the river cliff. Gen[l]. Neville possesses an island at its mouth, which stretches six miles down the Ohio and is a handsome farm.[2] After passing four or five islands off Indian's Logstown[3] 18 miles from Pittsburg, a gentleman from Salem and his lady with three children, had put off an hour before us in a family flat boat. As I had a boarding house acquaintance with him, I rowed myself forward in our skiff, and took coffee with him. As his boat was light, and he had two men who pretended to know the river, he said he should go on all night. The dangers of the river are *Planters, Sawyers* and *Wooden Isl-*

[1] Chartier's Creek flows into the Ohio three miles below Pittsburg. It received its name from a French-Shawnee half-breed who was a man of influence in his tribe about the middle of the eighteenth century. An Indian village, known as Chartier's Town, was situated at the mouth of the creek.

[2] General Neville's island was known commonly to Ohio navigators as Long Island. It lay immediately below Cow Island. Fortescue Cuming noted in 1807 that its soil was of the best quality and that it might be divided into several good farms. At that time Major Isaac Craig of Pittsburg had part of it under cultivation. After the close of the War of 1812 Major Craig retired to the island, where he resided until his death in 1826.

[3] Logstown was situated on a high bluff on the north bank of the Ohio, just below the site of the present town of Economy, Pennsylvania. During the middle of the eighteenth century it was the most important Indian trading village on the Pennsylvania frontier. Its population was a mixture of Iroquois, Mohican, and Shawnee. Soon after the establishment of Fort Duquesne in 1754, on the site of the later Pittsburg, the French built houses for the village's inhabitants, but after the early substitution of English for French supremacy in the region the place rapidly declined. Cuming, in 1807, speaks of it as "a scattering hamlet of four or five log cabins" (EARLY WESTERN TRAVELS, iv, p. 97).

ands.[1] A *Planter* is a tree rooted fast to the bottom of the river, & rotted off level with the water, a heavy boat striking one of them may be staved and sunk. *Sawyers* are trees less firmly rooted; they rise and fall with the water; if they point up the stream, they are dangerous, but not so much so when they point down. *Wooden Islands* are logs accumulated against planters or shoals.

On Friday the 20th we advanced 60 miles, passed Big beaver Creek, 70 yards wide at the mouth. Four miles up it has falls or rapids, which extend three miles. On them are forging, fulling, and grist mills; chiefly in the hands of Quakers. The river here is very crooked, bounded by high, precipitous, banks, which are covered with gigantic trees. In some places bare rocks project into the Stream, forming eddies and ripples. Beavertown,[2] a mis-

---

[1] " Planters are large bodies of trees firmly fixed by their roots in the bottom of the river, in a perpendicular manner, and appearing no more than about a foot above the surface of the water in its middling state. So firmly are they rooted, that the largest boat running against them, will not move them, but they frequently injure the boat.

" Sawyers are likewise bodies of trees fixed less perpendicularly in the river, and rather of a less size, yielding to the pressure of the current, disappearing and appearing by turns above the water, similar to the motion of a saw-mill saw, from which they have taken their name.

" Wooden-Islands are places where by some cause or other large quantities of driftwood have, through time, been arrested and matted together in different parts of the river." Zadoc Cramer, *The Ohio and Mississippi Navigator* (Pittsburg, 1804), p. 11. This little book, which passed through twelve editions, was the standard guide of navigators for more than a quarter of a century. There is a description and synopsis of it in Archer B. Hulbert, *Waterways of Westward Expansion* (HISTORIC HIGHWAYS OF AMERICA, ix, pp. 73-99).

[2] Big Beaver Creek, a stream about fifty yards wide at its mouth, flows into the Ohio ten miles below Logstown. The Indian vil-

erable place, was almost the only break we saw this day. It stands 200 feet above the river. The rounded pebbles evince that the Ohio has been 200 feet higher here, than it is now. We passed two or three log houses and taverns, with an acre or two of cleared land attached to each, but the general character of the river scenery is gloomy and grand. My amusement was to row the skiff through the eddies, to land and scramble up the rocks and search for curious plants or squirrels. This skiff is so light that I can with ease catch the boats when they are 3 miles ahead. I find that I have not forgotten the art of swimming, so that I am under no apprehension when the skiff strikes a log as it sometimes does.

I should have told you that I had a letter to Major N——, son of Gen. N——. This gentleman has shewn me much civility. His father was the richest man in Pensylvania, and has signalized himself

---

lage which was situated at its junction with the larger stream in the earlier part of the eighteenth century, where the town of Beaver now stands, was variously known as King Beaver's, Shinga's Old Town, or Sokhon. It was a noted station for the fur trade and frequently served as a base of operations in the border raids of the time. King Beaver, from whom the creek and settlement took their names, was the supreme chief of the Delawares — an ally of the English against the French until Braddock's defeat, but after that catastrophe a dangerous neutral, and in the end a leader in the Pontiac conspiracy. The present town of Beaver was laid out in 1792. Cuming says of it in 1807: "It stands on a stony plain on the top of the high cliff which conceals it from the river and contains about thirty indifferent houses, much scattered, on three parallel streets" (EARLY WESTERN TRAVELS, iv, p. 98). Flint, in 1818, says that within three miles of the mouth of the Beaver he found three saw-mills, a grist-mill, an iron furnace and forge, a fulling-mill, a carding-mill, and a mill for bruising flax-seed (EARLY WESTERN TRAVELS, ix, p. 95). These were the mills, of course, of which Fordham speaks.

in the Indian Wars. In M^r. N——'s house I found
books of taste; Ariosto, the English poets, &c &c,
which was quite refreshing after a long journey
through the wilds of Pensylvania. Major N. has
given me a letter to his father the General.

The inhabitants of the western towns are not so
hospitable as they were formerly. The constant
stream of emigration would make such hospitality
enormously expensive. Besides there are so many
unworthy characters amongst these emigrants, that
the people are become shy of them.

Saturday 21st. The hills are now rather lower,
and the woods a little more broken by settlements.
M^r. —— and ——, my fellow passengers, landed
at Wheeling,[1] which is the Court house town of

[1] The first building constructed on the site of Wheeling was
Fort Fincastle, a stockade erected during Lord Dunmore's war in
1774. The name of the structure was subsequently changed to
Fort Henry, in honor of Governor Patrick Henry of Virginia.
The first town lots at the place were laid out in 1783 by Colonel
Ebenezer Zane, who had taken up the land of the vicinity twenty-
three years before. In 1797 the town became the seat of Ohio
County, Virginia. At an early date Wheeling began to rival Pittsburg as a depot for westward commerce. Her advantage at first
lay simply in the fact that by shipping goods down the Ohio from
this point, rather than from Pittsburg, nearly a hundred miles
of the upper course of the river — the portion most difficult to
navigate in low water — were avoided. The only disadvantage was
that a day more was required to reach Wheeling from the East.
In 1818, when the Cumberland Road was completed to this place,
the obstacles of bad travel and delay were largely removed. The
new highway was the shortest route from Baltimore and Washington to the Ohio, and being in addition free from tolls until
it was ceded to the states in 1830-35, it became the great rival thoroughfare of the northern route by the Pennsylvania State Road.
Flint, in 1818, says that the carriage of goods was already cheaper
from Baltimore to Wheeling than from Philadelphia to Pittsburg (EARLY WESTERN TRAVELS, ix, p. 105). For descriptions of
Wheeling in the early part of the century see François André
Michaux, *Travels* (EARLY WESTERN TRAVELS, iii, p. 171); Fortescue
Cuming, *Sketches* (EARLY WESTERN TRAVELS, iv, p. 113); Thaddeus
M. Harris, *Journal* (EARLY WESTERN TRAVELS, iii, p. 349); Thomas

Ohio (the County, Virginia) and contains 120
houses 11 stores and 2 inns. I bought a tin pot for
boiling coffee for 62½ Cents. Several men were
drinking at the Tavern. At 9 A. M. this day it was
excessively hot. A shower fell, and the moisture
immediately rose off the plants in dense steam. We
moored at night below Fish Creek[1] five miles from
Wheeling, after having advanced 40 miles in the
day. As we were passing Fish Creek, our pratoon
pointed out a boat moored in the mouth of it, which
he said was D^r. B——'s. The skiff was directly
sent off and I jumped in. My greatest exertions could not prevent its being driven down
by the strength of the current about 100 yards,
as there was a counter current close in shore.
With some difficulty I got round the point into
the Creek. To my disappointment, it was not
the Doctor's boat. I then put off again; a bend
of the river was just taking the boats from my
sight, which were already a mile and a half
ahead. Evening was closing in—I rowed hard,
turned the bend, and the boats were out of sight. As
there were many islands, I was afraid of taking
the wrong current and passing the boats. The
darkness increased; I could not see either shore.
After shouting several times and rowing about half

Nuttall, *Journal* (EARLY WESTERN TRAVELS, xiii, p. 51); Adlard
Welby. *Visit to North America* (EARLY WESTERN TRAVELS, xii,
pp. 204-205); and John Woods, *Two Years' Residence* (EARLY
WESTERN TRAVELS, x, p. 221).

[1] For the connection of the Fish Creek region with the early
life of George Rogers Clark, see Thwaites (EARLY WESTERN
TRAVELS, iii, p. 350, note 37).

an hour, I heard voices in answer; and presently I saw a light. It was kindled on the deck of one of the boats, which was moored under the shade of some gigantic Sycamores. The sultry dark night — the croaking of the frogs — and the innumerable fireflies, which were flashing among the trees, all foretold a storm; which came on an hour after midnight. The lightning fell so near us, that we distinctly heard it whiz through the air. The trees, rocks, and hills were at times distinctly visible in the intense blaze, then lost in utter darkness; while the sky was rent by rattling thunder. The thunderstorms in England are insignificant to those of America.

Sunday the 22ᵈ. We made a short trip this day; — not quite 40 miles. The banks of the river here are exceedingly crooked, high, and crowned with dark forests.

Monday 23ᵈ. Landed at Marietta[1] at 9 A. M., a

---

[1] Marietta is located at the junction of the Muskingum and the Ohio, about sixty miles below Wheeling. The town dates from 1788 and, unlike most of the settlements of the Ohio Valley, had its origin in migration from New England rather than from the southern states. In 1786 a group of soldiers who were interested in securing the bounty lands due them for service in the Revolution organized at Boston what was known as the Ohio Company, with a view to getting possession of a considerable tract of land in the territory northwest of the Ohio. As soon as the Northwest Ordinance was enacted, in 1787, the company designated Dr. Manasseh Cutler to make the necessary contract with Congress. The result was an arrangement for the purchase of 1,500,000 acres at 66 2-3 cents per acre. At a meeting of the company in Boston, August 30, 1787, it was voted that 5,760 acres about the mouth of the Muskingum should be reserved for a town and commons. In November of the same year twenty-two mechanics set out from Danvers, Massachusetts, to begin preparations for the new settlement, and within a twelvemonth a town of considerable proportions had been laid out and given a very respectable population. The site chosen was on the left bank of the Muskingum, opposite Fort Harmar — a stronghold constructed

pretty town on the banks of the Muskingham, having about 120 houses. This town is laid out on rather a large scale, which will not be filled up for a century or more. The streets are now green lanes, bounded by worm fences. Where houses ought to be, there are now groves or gardens. The land is good, and pretty well cultivated. Here I found D^r. B., whose men were going to leave him. He wished me much to take the command of his boat, which I declined, as I did not like to leave my luggage. I, however, found and engaged two sailors for him.

The banks of the Ohio are now comparatively low and fertile, both on the Ohio and Kentucky side, but most so on that of the latter state. They are not yet more than broken into by the axe of the cultivator. The Muskingham is a fine river. It is crossed by a ferry boat, attached to a cable stretched high above the water, alternately at the head and stern of the ferry boat it is carried over either

in 1785-86 by a detachment of troops under Major John Doughty to afford protection to the Virginia frontiers. The name first given the New England settlement was Adelphi, but this was soon changed to Marietta, in honor of the queen of France, Marie Antoinette, whose gracious reception of Franklin at court was just then the subject of admiring comment throughout America. The town did not grow as its founders hoped it would, chiefly because the rich interior of Ohio offered immigrants too many counter attractions. For a description of the place in 1802 see F. A. Michaux, *Travels* (EARLY WESTERN TRAVELS, iii, p. 177); in 1807, Cuming, *Sketches* (EARLY WESTERN TRAVELS, iv, p. 124); in 1811, Melish, *Travels*, ii, pp. 101-107; in 1818, Flint, *Letters* (EARLY WESTERN TRAVELS, ix, p. 109), and Evans, *Pedestrious Tour* (EARLY WESTERN TRAVELS, viii, p. 264); and in 1820, Woods, *Two Years' Residence* (EARLY WESTERN TRAVELS, x, p. 223). Thomas J. Summers, *History of Marietta* (Marietta, 1903) is useful. There is an interesting plan of Marietta in 1803 in Thaddeus M. Harris, *Journal*, which is reproduced in Winsor, *The Westward Movement*, p. 303.

way by the force of the current.[1]   This evening M[r].
P—— and I went forward in the skiff to examine a
cave near the mouth of Shade river; but this river
is so concealed by rocks and trees, that we passed
it without seeing it, and we were unable to row
back before the boats came down.

As the late rains have made the waters uncom-
monly high, our pratoon held on all night.   On
Tuesday we passed Blannerhasset's Island.[2]   The
Estate the proprietor forfeited on account of some

---

[1] This ferry was noted and described by almost every traveller
who visited Marietta, for example, by Thomas Hulme, *Journal*
(EARLY WESTERN TRAVELS, x, p. 40).

[2] Blennerhassett's Island lies eighteen miles below Marietta and
two below the mouth of the Little Kanawha and the present city
of Parkersburg, West Virginia.   It is three and a half miles in
length and contains about 500 acres of very fertile land.   Harman
Blennerhassett, from whom the island takes its name, was an
Irishman of wealth and refinement who migrated to the United
States out of admiration for American democratic government and
society.   In 1798 he bought the island below the Little Kanawha
and there established his family in a home which soon became
noted as a centre of culture and good manners.   In 1805 the
Blennerhassetts were visited by Aaron Burr, then on his way to
New Orleans, and unfortunately the gifted proprietor was so attracted by the questionable schemes of the plotter that he committed himself unreservedly to them and staked his whole fortune
upon their success.   In little more than a year the bubble had
burst, Burr was a refugee, and Blennerhassett had been himself
compelled to seek safety in flight.   Both men were arrested and
tried for treason, but, on technical grounds, acquitted.   In the
meantime the Blennerhassett estate was overrun by hungry credi-
tors and seriously impaired in value.   In 1811 the fine mansion,
with all the art treasures and books it contained, was ruined by
an accidental fire, and thereafter little was left to tell of the
splendor of the place in its happier days.   Blennerhassett himself eked out a pitiable existence as a virtual outlaw and exile
until his death, on the Island of Guernsey, in 1831.   Cuming,
in his *Sketches,* gives a very interesting description of the Blennerhassett estate as it appeared in 1807 (EARLY WESTERN TRAVELS,
iv, pp. 128-130); and Melish (*Travels,* ii, p. 109) describes it in its
deserted condition in 1811.   For an account of the island as it
is to-day see Thwaites, *On the Storied Ohio,* pp. 95-98.

attempt which he made to excite an insurrection against the government of the United States. Galliopagus[1] was the next village, which struck my fancy. It was founded by a hundred French families, about 30 years ago, on the Ohio side. Their title was a bad one, and all who were not rich enough to purchase their estates a second time were ejected. The place has not flourished since, although its site is most beautiful.

On Wednesday we moored at Portsmouth[2] 390

[1] The writer means Gallipolis. This town is on the right bank of the Ohio, nearly opposite the mouth of the Great Kanawha. It is about one hundred miles below Marietta. The early history of Gallipolis was extremely unfortunate, as Fordham suggests. The Scioto Company, an off-shoot of the Ohio Company, proposed to reap a harvest by disposing of its western lands to discontented inhabitants of France, and in 1788 sent an agent to Paris in the person of the poet Joel Barlow to advertize the attractions of the American West and to stimulate emigration thither. Barlow executed his commission faithfully, with the result that in 1790 about six hundred French people — of every type but that adapted to frontier life — arrived *en route* at Alexandria, Virginia. There the prospective settlers were compelled to tarry fifteen months, to await the termination of Indian uprisings on the Ohio and to secure new land titles as far as possible, in the place of worthless ones which the Company had tricked them into accepting. After the emigrants finally arrived on the Scioto they proved totally unable to cope with the hardships of backwoods existence. By granting them 20,000 acres of land between the mouth of the Sandy and Scioto rivers Congress endeavored to make amends for the Company's swindle, and the thirty families who removed to this tract, settling at the mouth of the Great Scioto, succeeded for a time fairly well. But Gallipolis was an absolute failure, and, but for the coming in of American settlers, would likely have been completely extinguished. There is to-day almost no trace of the town's French origin. F. A. Michaux, in his *Travels,* says that in 1807 the settlement was composed of sixty log-houses, mostly uninhabited and falling to pieces, the remainder occupied by Frenchmen " who breathe out a miserable existence" (EARLY WESTERN TRAVELS, iii, p. 184). Melish (*Travels,* ii, pp. 115-117) gives the place, in 1811, a population of 300. See "Centennial of Gallipolis," in Ohio Archæological and Historical Society *Publications,* iii.

[2] Portsmouth, at the mouth of the Scioto, was laid out in 1803 by Henry Massie, taking its name from Portsmouth, Virginia.

miles from Pittsburg. The men at the oars of the second boat, Germans and Swiss, not understanding the orders of the Pratoon, pulled it into a current they were unable to stem, and it was driven against a tree with a tremendous crash. It was loaded with Iron, and had my luggage on board. It got off with no material damage, except being stripped of one of its roofs. Whilst the attention of our people was called off to that boat, we were drifting on a Planter, the point of which projected about a foot above the water. Our Pratoon called the men to their duty; but though the boat cleared it, one oar, made of an entire tree, caught against the stump. The men dropped down to save themselves; I had that moment, thrown myself on the oar to assist them. Its recoil threw me into the boat, with no injury but a slight contusion on the thigh.

After we had moored at Portsmouth, Mess[rs]. P—— C—— and myself went to the mouth of the Scioto, and then into the skiff, to see the ancient Indian fort opposite Alexandria.[1] The Shawanees,

---

The surrounding region, being a noted rendezvous of the Shawnees, had long been resorted to with frequency by French and English fur-traders. Travellers generally speak well of the town in its early years. Cuming (*Sketches*) tells us, in 1807, that though it contained as yet but twenty houses it had a handsome and healthy situation and, as the seat of Scioto County, was likely to grow to be a place of some importance (EARLY WESTERN TRAVELS, iv, p. 161). Flint (*Letters from America*) says, in 1818, that it was well-built and had a court house, a newspaper office, a woollen factory, a number of stores, and several good taverns (EARLY WESTERN TRAVELS, ix, p. 113). See Thwaites, *On the Storied Ohio*, pp. 151-154.

[1] Alexandria is situated on the western bank of the Scioto, opposite Portsmouth. The town was founded by Major John Belli,

though not the first constructors of the fort, which is a circular redoubt, were defeated here by Gen. St. Clair[1] 35 years ago, and have since descended the Mississippi. After a charming ramble of an hour, we attempted the arduous task of rowing, poling, and dragging the skiff up the stream about two miles and a half. The flood had run in among the trees, and the eddies and counter-currents helped

an Englishman who settled at Alexandria, Virginia, in 1783, and who, after 1791, interested himself in the development of the Ohio country. The site of Alexandria was occupied in the first half of the eighteenth century by the chief town of the Shawnees — the place at which, in March, 1751, Christopher Gist was warned back while inspecting lands for the Ohio Company. In 1753 a flood led the Shawnees to abandon the place. Some of them sought new homes in regions further north, while others established a new village across the Scioto, on the site of Portsmouth. Cuming, returning from his western tour in 1807, visited Belli's new town, subsequently recording in his *Sketches*: "This village . . . is nicknamed Hardscramble, either from the hilly roads by which one arrives at it, or from the difficulty experienced by the first settlers to obtain a subsistence. It contains about a dozen houses and cabins, a meeting house, and three taverns, but does not seem to thrive" (EARLY WESTERN TRAVELS, iv, p. 237). The fort to which Fordham refers was across the Ohio, on the Kentucky shore, on the site of the present Springville.

[1] General Arthur St. Clair was a Scotchman who came to America in 1755 with Admiral Boscowen. He served in Canada under General Wolfe in 1759-60 and after the close of the war was placed in command of Fort Ligonier in Pennsylvania. He had an honorable career in the Revolution, rising to the rank of major-general, and rendering Washington valued service in the Yorktown campaign. In 1786 he was elected a member of the Continental Congress from Pennsylvania, and the following year he became president of that body, now about to expire. When the Northwest Territory was organized under the Ordinance of 1787 he was made its first governor. In this office he remained until 1802, when Ohio was on the point of being constituted a state. In 1790 occurred one of the periodic movements of the Indians of the West to expel the whites. General Harmar was ordered to conduct the campaign against the redskins, but being at least partially defeated in the Maumee country, he was replaced after a few months by St. Clair. September 17, 1791, the new commander set out from Fort Washington (on the site of Cincinnati) for the country about Detroit; but on November 4 he was surprised and totally defeated on the banks of a small

us, but so often was the skiff bumped against logs,
that M^r. C. preferred walking on shore and dragging the rope when he could. In two hours and a
half we got up the river, high enough to cross over
to Portsmouth. With two oars and two paddles,
we worked as hard as three young men in high
spirits could work. We dashed across in the midst
of floating logs and branches of trees, which the
river was bringing down in great abundance.

Thursday ——. A heavy thunderstorm and rain
kept us within this morning. Called at Manchester,[1] a village of 25 houses in the State of Ohio.
Here, as in all the Ohio towns, the people are rude
and half civilized, yet very sharp and inquisitive.

We reached at length the pleasant thriving town
of Maysville,[2] Adam's County, Kentucky. Here

tributary of the Wabash. St. Clair retired from command in
chagrin, popular sentiment generally holding him at fault. He
was succeeded by General Wayne, who defeated the Indians in
August, 1794, and concluded a lasting peace with them at Greenville, Ohio, a year later. After yielding the governorship of the
Northwest Territory in 1802, St. Clair lived in obscurity in Pennsylvania until his death in 1818.

[1]Manchester is in Adams County, Ohio, twelve miles above
Maysville. It was laid out in 1791 by Nathaniel Massie, a surveyor of bounty lands, and was the pioneer Virginia settlement on
the north bank of the Ohio. The town's growth was very slow.
Cuming (*Sketches*) says that in 1807 it had only ten houses and
was not likely to thrive, owing to the proximity of Maysville,
Kentucky (EARLY WESTERN TRAVELS, iv, p. 167).

[2]Maysville, in the earlier years of its history, was commonly
known as Limestone, from the quantity of rock of that variety
found in the neighborhood. The first building upon its site was
a blockhouse erected in 1783. The town may be said to have been
settled the following year, and in 1787 it was incorporated by the
Virginia legislature. F. A. Michaux (*Travels*) says, in 1802,
that it had thirty or forty houses of wood; that it had long been
the place where all emigrants by way of Pittsburg and the Ohio
landed; and that it was still the staple for all sorts of mer-

the tall, pale, well dressed men, and agreeable looking women, reminded me of Virginia, of which
Kentucky is an offslip. There are a few slaves in
this place, comfortable, sleek looking fellows. We
entered the port in the afternoon, amid repeated
feux de joie from some small pieces of cannon. On
enquiring the cause, we learnt that a vessel from
Baltimore had just arrived with Gen. N. from New
Orleans, and several from Pittsburg, and on this
account they were firing. I smiled at the cause, yet
I could not but admire the effect of this cannonade.
The echoes rolled along the high banks like claps of
thunder.

The dislike of Slavery is becoming less violent.
There are more men of refined manners and cultivated minds in the slave states, than in those that
are more consistently democratic. This I learn
more from information than observation; yet both
more and more confirm me in this opinion. Behind
this town is a fine, rocky, eminence, up to which we
scrambled through a watercourse. On the top, we
were rewarded for our trouble by a birds-eye view
of the Town, and the river of Limestone Creek, as

chandise sent from Philadelphia and Baltimore to Kentucky (EARLY
WESTERN TRAVELS, iii, p. 195). The distance from Maysville to
Lexington was only sixty-five miles by the road running through
the present Mason, Fleming, Nicholas, Bourbon, and Fayette
counties, by way of Mayslick, Millersburg, and Paris. Cuming
(*Sketches*) says, in 1807, that the place was not growing and
existed merely on the traffic passing through it, but that it was
the greatest shipping port on the Ohio below Pittsburg — the port
for northeastern Kentucky as Louisville was for the southwestern
part of that state (EARLY WESTERN TRAVELS, iv, p. 169). Other
characterizations may be found in Flint, *Letters* (EARLY WESTERN
TRAVELS, ix, pp. 127-131) and in Welby, *Visit to North America,*
(EARLY WESTERN TRAVELS, xii, pp. 214-218).

rich and beautiful as can be imagined. The top of
the hill is a rich, black, earth, producing abundant
crops of Indian corn and wheat: the latter is changing colour. . . .

In two days I shall see my friends in Cincinnati,
from whom I have been separated seven weeks to-
day; and I have travelled in that time 1200 miles.

Saturday. Left the pretty town of Augusta;[1]
went to Gen. N——'s villa with a letter from his
son. I spent great part of the day with this fine old
gentleman and his amiable family. . . .

We moored in the course of the day seven miles
from Cincinnati. If a thundergust had not occurred, I should have gone thither in the skiff, but
it was not possible. So I rolled about in my blanket
all night, called the Pratoon before day, tugged at
the oar with the men, and got to Cincinnati[2] early
in the morning. I saw —— and the rest of the
party, who are all well and happy.

---

[1] Augusta, once the seat of justice of Bracken County, Kentucky,
is about twenty miles below Maysville and forty-two above Cincinnati. It is important only as a shipping point for tobacco.
Woods (*Two Years' Residence*) tells us, in 1820, that the town
was established to rival Maysville in the back-country trade and
that "it appears a flourishing place" (Early Western Travels,
x, p. 233).

[2] On Cincinnati, see p. 183, note.

V

St Vincennes State of Indiana
July 26. 1817.

I WROTE to C—— as I descended the Ohio, and finished my letter at Cincinnati and sent it thence to Philadelphia. I hope it has been received safe by this time, for I had great pleasure in writing it, and often pictured to myself your family circle, gathered together in the garden parlour, listening to the narrative of the journeyings of their poor wanderer. . . .

I cannot give you a journal of our march across Indiana: many sheets of paper could not contain it; and I am too well employed in business or too much engaged in the pleasures of the chase, to devote much time to writing. Do not take this confession unkindly; if I am wrong, I have many excuses and palliatives to offer; — but I know you will excuse me.

We travelled on horseback, each person furnished with an upper and under blanket, and saddle-bags, and two pack horses with extra luggage and bedding. Taverns on the road are bad and "few and far between." Farmers have generally a room appropriated to the reception of travellers, for whose food they charge moderately. We were furnished with guns and tomohawks, and all things necessary to encamp in the woods; which M[r]. B. actually did one night; but the main body of the party escaped that adventure.

Indiana is a vast forest, larger than England, just penetrated in places, by the back-wood settlers, who are half hunters, half farmers.[1]

This old town, which was a settlement made by the Indian traders, stands near the river on a beautiful prairie, surrounded by woods and gently rising hills. Its inhabitants are Canadian and European French, Anglo Americans, Negroes, and a few half-bre[e]d Indians. The French have given their tone of manners to the place.[2]

There are many Indians in the neighborhood, Delawares, Miamies, and Kaskaskians. The for-

---

[1] Birkbeck gives a reasonably full account of the expedition of his party (including Fordham) across southern Indiana. His observations on the people and resources of the state, if cursory, are yet interesting. See *Notes on a Journey in America*, pp. 90-98.

[2] The founding of Vincennes has been assigned to various years between 1702 and 1735. The most probable date is the latter, though it appears that François Morgan, Sieur de Vincennes, at the command of Governor Perier of Louisiana, visited the site of the future town as early as 1727 and erected a fort to counteract the designs of the English on the Indian trade of the Wabash Valley. But the first authenticated settlement of Frenchmen with their families occurred in 1735. When George Croghan visited the town thirty years later he found it to contain eighty or ninety French families —"an idle, lazy people, a parcel of renegadoes from Canada, much worse than the Indians." *Tours into the Western Country* (EARLY WESTERN TRAVELS, i, pp. 141-142). Faux, in 1819, says in his *Memorable Days* that although long the capital and mother-town of the state, Vincennes looked like an "old, worn-out, dirty village of wooden frame houses, which a fire might much improve" (EARLY WESTERN TRAVELS, xi, p. 207). Welby (*Visit to North America*) gives an interesting account of a sojourn at the place in 1819 (EARLY WESTERN TRAVELS, xii, pp. 236-248). The generally unfavorable comments of the travellers may be off-set and incidentally explained somewhat by the following statement of Birkbeck (*Notes*, p. 105), in 1817: "There is nothing in Vincennes, on its first appearance, to make a favourable im-

mer tribe contains about 1200 warriors, and are a fierce, determined race of men. The Miamies and Kaskaskians, though excellent warriors, are more mild. They all hunt and fight with rifles, and are good marksmen. I have seen a young Delaware warrior present a heavy rifle, and hold it immovable without a rest, for several minutes. Some of the Miamies are very fine fellows; comparatively rich. Their Tomohawks and guns are beautifully ornamented. They ride blood ponies; and some of them have handsome saddles and bridles.[1]

I have received an invitation to visit a camp of Miamies, a few miles hence, and to join a hunting party. I have declined it, not being master of sufficient leisure, nor do I know enough of the Indian, who invited me, to entrust myself with them.

We staid at St. Vincennes a week, then went 25 miles S. W. to a little new town, called Princetown,[2] of about 20 houses, situated in the woods. We like the place so much that a house is hired for 9 months

pression on a stranger; but it improves on acquaintance, for it contains agreeable people: and there is a spirit of cleanliness, and even neatness in their houses and manner of living: there is also a strain of politeness, which marks the origin of this settlement in a way very flattering to the French." The development of Vincennes will be found well treated in the histories of Indiana by Dillon, Dunn, and William H. Smith, and in Hubbard M. Smith's *Historical Sketches of Old Vincennes* (Vincennes, 1902).

[1] Birkbeck gives a valuable description of the Indians of the Vincennes region in his *Notes*, pp. 99-100.

[2] Princeton is situated about thirty miles south of Vincennes, within two miles of the Patoka River and ten of the Wabash. The first settlement in the vicinity was made as early as 1800. In 1813 Gibson County was erected and Princeton became its seat. Town lots were first put on sale in 1814. The place received its name from William Prince, an Indian agent located there in 1812, subsequently a member of Congress. Hulme (*Journal*)

and there the ladies, servants, and myself are left, while M^r. B—— & —— go on to explore.

I have met with two agreeable men, of whom I have heard excellent characters, and who have shown me great civilities. M^r. H—— and Col. E—— a gentleman from Virginia. The latter, especially, is a very engaging man; just after my own heart. All I have heard of him has been favorable, and the best of it has been confirmed to me by Gen. —— an old revolutionary officer.

Col. E—— and M^r. H—— have proposed to form a grand hunting party, as soon as I shall be at leisure; and Judge P—— with several experienced hunters are to go with us. We shall be out several days. Our game will be deer, bears, and opossums.

My health is good. I never sleep in a bed: usually my cloak and saddle-blanket, spread on the floor, form my couch. The climate is so fine, that sleeping in open balconies is a common practice.

I left Princetown yesterday, accompanied by —— in order to copy a map of the Southern part of the State of Indiana from the Maps of the Land Office. I shall most probably finish it, and return, tomorrow.

---

speaks of it in 1818 as a very dull town and says it will never be otherwise while *all* the inhabitants persist in attempting to be keepers of stores and taverns (EARLY WESTERN TRAVELS, x, p. 46). Faux (*Memorable Days*) gives an account of a sojourn there a few years after Hulme's visit (EARLY WESTERN TRAVELS, xi, pp. 214-224). For a noteworthy word-picture of the development of little frontier towns of the type of Princeton, see Birkbeck, *Notes*, pp. 104-105. The families of Birkbeck and Flower were left at Princeton in the autumn of 1817, while the Illinois prairies were being examined and places of habitation prepared.

M^r. B., after he returns from the Illinois territory, wishes minutely to survey the banks of the Ohio, from the Wabash to the Great Miami.

Best land is worth 6 or 700£ sterling per section: further from Market 350£ or 400£ — uncleared.

Let important letters have duplicates, and even triplicates, sent by different ships, and with different directions.

VI

The forests of Indiana — The Indiana Constitution — Character and prices of land — Emigration directed further west — Commercial importance of the Mississippi — Unhealthy conditions on the lower Mississippi — The Wabash — Description of Princeton — Prospective visit to the Illinois Territory.

July 31. 1817.

Princetown, Gibson County, Indiana.

. . . We left Cincinnati in the last week in June, and crossed over the Great Miami River into Indiana. Excepting on the banks of the Rivers Ohio and Wabash, this state is one vast forest, intersected by a few *Blaze* roads[1] and two or three open roads. There are a few new towns, and some settlements on and near the state roads and rivers. These are generally from one to three years old; though there are much older and more substantial improvements on the Ohio; and St Vincennes on the Wabash was settled 30 years ago. Indiana has been a state only two years. Its constitution seems to have exhausted the wisdom of all ages and countries — so complete is it — and yet so simple. It has a Governor, who is President in the Senate, and Commander in Chief of its armies; a Lieutenant Governor; a Senate; a Legislative body; and is represented in Congress by two members. Its Executive [*sic*] consists of Cir-

---

[1] Blaze roads are merely lines, marked through the forests by slices of bark, like a *blaze,* being chopped off the trees. When a road is surveyed, the trees are cut down, and the stumps are left to rot in the ground. The trees on each side are notched at convenient distances, to distinguish the State road from private ones to Plantations, and this is then called an open road.
—FORDHAM.

cuit Courts, and a Supreme Court. Its civil code is founded on the Common Law of England. Every office, civil or military, is elective, and held only during good behaviour. Every citizen is by law a soldier, but he need not enter the regular army unless he choose it. Every Citizen may carry what arms he please for the defence of his person or property. Slavery is not allowed in this State. All religions are equally protected. The word "tolerate" is not to be found in the articles of their Constitution.[1]

The land near the Water Courses is excellent. Some of the very first quality; but all that is quite conveniently situated on the Ohio banks, that is,

[1] There is a similar synopsis of the Indiana system of government in William Tell Harris's *Tour Through the United States,* pp. 136-137. The main steps in the organization of civil government in Indiana may be indicated briefly. In 1800 Congress made a division of the Northwest Territory, creating a separate Indiana Territory which comprised practically all of the original except Ohio. The capital was fixed at Vincennes, and William Henry Harrison was appointed the first governor. In 1805 Congress attached to Indiana the "District of Louisiana"—all possessions west of the Mississippi and north of 33°; but this great region was detached again in the following year. In 1805, also, the Michigan Territory was given a separate organization. The first general assembly of the Indiana Territory met at Vincennes July 29, 1805. In 1809 the Territory was once more pared down, Illinois being separated from it. By 1810 the population of Indiana proper was 24,520. In 1813 the legislature moved the territorial capital from Vincennes to Corydon, on the Ohio. In 1815 the legislature petitioned Congress for the admission of Indiana as a state, alleging that the Territory now had a population of nearly 67,000. In the enabling act which resulted, in 1816, Congress granted the forthcoming state four sections of land to be acquired from the Indians for a new seat of government. The legislature appointed a commission to select a site, and after a time Indianapolis was chosen, though as yet the place was but a wilderness more than sixty miles from so much as a store; the capital was not transferred thither until 1825. In pursuance of the enabling act a convention of delegates met at Corydon, June 10, 1816, and framed the constitution concerning whose features Fordham speaks.

7

high, dry, and rich, has been already entered. It was bought at the auctions of the U. S. at high prices, from 10 to 15$ p^r. acre. What was not then sold may now be purchased at 2$ p^r. acre at the Land Offices; but it is often better to give 6 or 7$ per acre to the first settler for his chosen section with an improvement upon it, than to go into the woods, away from a navigable river and take land at the Land Office price.[1] You have not a bad

---

[1] The earliest arrangements for the sale of public land were effected by an ordinance of 1785, which established the quadrangular section of 640 acres as the unit. During the next eleven years — a period of great activity on the part of speculating land companies — there remained no provision for the sale of land in small quantities, and only after 1796 could a single section of 640 acres be disposed of to a purchaser. Even this modification did not open the public domain to the would-be land-holder who was poor. In 1799 William Henry Harrison, who had been Secretary of the Northwest Territory under the governorship of General St. Clair, was elected by the general assembly of the Territory to the office of delegate to Congress. Being appointed chairman of the House committee on public lands, Harrison gave his attention to drafting and securing the passage of an act authorizing the sale of public land in half-sections, or tracts of 320 acres. By this act (1800) it was further provided that only one-fourth of the purchase price need be paid down, while for the rest credit of two, three and four years was to be given. This act was properly regarded as a great public boon, for its tendency was to open the public domain to the worthy but poor emigrant — to give farms to the many instead of plantations to the few. The process of paring down the saleable units went on in after years, until in our own day it has been possible to gain a title to as small an area as forty acres. The method by which public land was divided and sold in the period in which Fordham wrote is described with admirable clearness by Flint, in his *Letters from America*, as follows: "In the public land-offices, maps of the new lands are kept. Sections of a square mile, and quarter sections of 160 acres, are laid down. The squares entered are marked A. P. meaning advance paid. This advance is half a dollar per acre, or one-fourth of the price. Lands, when first put to sale, are offered by public auction, and are set up at two dollars per acre. If no one offers that price, they are exhibited on the land-office map, and may be sold at that rate at any subsequent time. Besides the land-offices for the sale of national property, there are agents who sell on account of individuals. I can mention Mr. Embree, of Cincinnati, as a gentleman who does much business in this way, and with

chance, however, in this latter plan, for there is a
district as large as all England to be picked over
now. M^r. —— and I have a great fancy to look

much reputation to himself. Lands entered at the public sales,
or at the Register's office, are payable, one fourth part of the
price at the time of purchase; one fourth at the expiry of two
years; one fourth at three years, and the remaining fourth at
four years. By law, lands not fully paid at the end of five years,
are forfeited to the government, but examples are not wanting
of States petitioning Congress for indulgence on this point, and
obtaining it. For money paid in advance at the land office a dis-
count of eight per cent. per annum is allowed, till instalments to
the amount of the payment become due. For failures in the
payment of instalments, interest at six per cent. is taken till paid.
The most skilful speculators usually pay only a fourth part of the
price at entry, conceiving that they can derive a much greater
profit than eight per cent. per annum from the increasing value
of property, and occasionally from renting it out to others. Where
judicious selections are made, they calculate rightly. The land
system now adopted in the United States is admirable in regard
to ingenuity, simplicity, and liberality. A slight attention to
the map of the district, will enable any one to know at once the
relative situation of any section that he may afterwards hear
mentioned, and its direct distance in measured miles. There can
be no necessity for giving names to farms or estates, as the
designation of the particular township, and the number of the
section is sufficient, and has, besides, the singular convenience of
conveying accurate information as to where it is situated. By
the new arrangement the boundaries of possessions are most
securely fixed, and freed alike from the inconvenience of rivers
changing their course, and complexity of curved lines. Litigation
amongst neighbors as to their landmarks, is in a great measure
excluded. The title deed is printed on a piece of parchment of
the quarto size. The date, the locality of the purchase, and the
purchaser's name, are inserted in writing, and the instrument is
subscribed by the President of the United States, and the agent
of the general land office. It is delivered to the buyer free of all
expense, and may be transferred by him to another person without
using stamped paper, and without the intervention of a law prac-
titioner. The business of the land office proceeds on the most
moderate principles, and with the strictest regard to justice. The
proceeds are applied in defraying the expense of government,
and form a resource against taxation. The public lands are in
reality the property of the people. The stranger who would go
into the woods to make a selection of lands, ought to take with
him an extract from the land office map applying to the part of
the country he intends to visit. Without this, he cannot well
distinguish entered from unentered grounds. He should also
procure the names of the resident people, with the numbers and
quarters of the sections they live on, not neglecting to carry

at the Western side of the Illinois territory; and since he and Mᵣ. B—— have left me here, I have received an account of a tract of land on the left bank of the Mississippi, reaching from Kaskaskia[1] nearly to Sᵗ. Louis. It is called the American bottom, and consists of rich Alluvium from 8 to 40 feet deep. There is a farm to be sold there of 1400

with him a pocket-compass, to enable him to follow the blazed lines marked out by the surveyor. *Blaze* is a word signifying a mark cut by a hatchet on the bark of a tree. It is the more necessary for the explorer to be furnished thus, as he may expect to meet with settlers who will not be willing to direct him, but, on the contrary, tell him with the greatest effrontery, that every neighbouring quarter section is already taken up. Squatters, a class of men who take possession without purchasing, are afraid of being turned out, or of having their pastures abridged by new comers. Others, perhaps meditating an enlargement of their property, so soon as funds will permit, wish to hold the adjoining lands in reserve for themselves, and not a few are jealous of the land-dealer, who is not an actual settler, whose grounds lie waste, waiting for that advance on the value of property, which arises from an increasing population. The non-resident proprietor is injurious to a neighbourhood, in respect of his not bearing any part of the expense of making roads, while other people are frequently under the necessity of making them through his lands for their own convenience. On excursions of this kind, the prudent will always be cautious of explaining their views, particularly as to the spot chosen for purchase and without loss of time they should return to the land-office and make entry" (EARLY WESTERN TRAVELS, ix, pp. 175-181). Woods (*Two Years' Residence*), in 1820, has a good account, similar to Flint's (EARLY WESTERN TRAVELS, x, pp. 330-334).

[1] Kaskaskia was situated on the east bank of the Kaskaskia River, four miles east of the Mississippi. It was about 150 miles distant from Vincennes. The town owed its origin to the migration of French traders and missionaries thither about 1700, induced by the removal of the Kaskaskia tribe of Indians to the region at that time. It continued a straggling settlement of coureurs des bois and Indians until taken possession of by the English in 1765. In 1772, after the abandonment of Fort Chartres, Kaskaskia became the "capital" of the Illinois country. In 1778 it was captured from the English by George Rogers Clark during the course of his notable campaigns in the West. It remained the capital of Illinois until 1821, when it was succeeded in that dignity by the wilderness town of Vandalia. The village was all but ruined by a flood in 1844, and in 1847 it ceased even to be the seat of Randolph County.

acres, with house and buildings, for 5$ p^r. acre; the land, half prairie, half wood, and all richer than your tame, English, imagination can conceive; at least, if it be equal to the descriptions I have of it.[1] The wave of Emigration has already reached 200 miles up the Missouri. It is this thirst, this rapacious desire, to obtain the very best land, that keeps Indiana so thinly inhabited.

If the whole population of England were planted in Indiana and Illinois, there would be good land enough in the state and territory to make every man an independent farmer.

Were the choice left to me, I would settle on the Ohio banks below the falls,[2] or on the Missis-

---

[1] The American Bottom lay between a range of hills and the Mississippi, extending from the Kaskaskia on the south to the mouth of the Missouri on the north. Its length was about 100 miles and its area something like 320,000 acres, embracing present Monroe and St. Clair counties, with parts of Randolph and Madison. It is the most extended unbroken stretch of fertile prairie in Illinois and had the reputation in the early nineteenth century of being the richest agricultural land in the United States. It contained the first white settlements in Illinois — the French posts of Kaskaskia, Cahokia, and Prairie du Rocher. Its name was given it when it constituted the western boundary of the United States, before the acquisition of Louisiana.

[2] The "falls" of the Ohio comprise a stretch of rapids between Louisville and the present suburb Shippingport, two and a half miles down stream. A ledge of rocks extending across the river produces in this distance a descent of about twenty-five feet, rendering steam-boat navigation impossible except at high water and the passage of other craft more or less hazardous at all times. Until a canal was completed around the falls in 1830 it was generally necessary for the cargoes of all boats to be unloaded at one end, transported by land to the other end, and there reloaded for the remainder of the voyage. The local employment thus afforded laborers, and the desirability of distributing goods thence as far as possible without a second loading on the river craft, inevitably gave rise to a town, which in time grew into the city of Louisville. The Ohio Falls were noted and described by nearly every traveller in the West, beginning with Croghan in 1765.

sippi, — that "father of waters," as the Indians call it, below its junction with the Missouri; because that great river must be as much the high road of Commerce as Main Street is in Philadelphia, or Cheapside in London. Every kind of produce is sent to New Orleans in the cheapest way — to Europe if you please, or to the West Indies, for Sea vessels are often built on the river, but flat boats are the usual conveyances. For the conveyance of goods up the river, keel boats are used which are impelled by sails, oars and poles. Steam boats are now beginning to supersede their use, and one of 400 tons burden has made several trips.[1]

Melish, in 1811, has a good account, accompanied by an excellent map of the vicinity, in his *Travels*, ii, pp. 149-152. Descriptions by Nuttall (*Journal*) in 1818, EARLY WESTERN TRAVELS, xiii, p. 66; Hulme (*Journal*) in 1818, EARLY WESTERN TRAVELS, x, p. 43; and Woods (*Two Years' Residence*) in 1820, EARLY WESTERN TRAVELS, x, pp. 242-243, are of value. H. McMurtrie's *Sketches of Louisville and its Environs* (Louisville, 1819) contains a good description and map. The long-discussed project of constructing a canal around the falls was revived in 1804 and in that year a company to undertake the work was incorporated by the legislature of Kentucky. Owing, however, to the indifference of Louisville (whose prosperity was thought to depend largely on the continuance of the rehandling of goods occasioned by the lack of a canal) and other causes, nothing further was done until 1825. In that year a new organization, the Louisville and Portland Canal Company, was chartered, with a capital of $600,000. It was this company which, during the next five years, pushed the project to completion. The canal was enlarged in 1872, and in 1874, by act of Congress, it passed under the control of the United States.

[1] The first steamboat to appear on the Ohio was the *New Orleans* (built by Nicholas J. Roosevelt in 1810) which in 1811 descended to the city from which she took her name. In 1815 the *Aetna* led the way in stemming the current from New Orleans to Louisville. Thereafter steamboat navigation on the Ohio and the Mississippi developed steadily — to such a degree, in fact, that within a few years Wheeling, Marietta, Pittsburg, Cincinnati, and Louisville came to number shipbuilding among their most important industries. In 1818 fourteen steamers were built in these

Again — the Mississippi banks below the Ohio mouth are universally unhealthy, generally uninhabitable, from the overflowing of the River and the many Bayous which form inland swamps of great extent. The perpendicular rise of the river water is sometimes 200 feet, at such times the whole valley of the Mississippi below the Ohio is overflowed. Now this is not the case above the Ohio. The Bluffs of Kaskaskia are always safe. How valuable then must land be in such situations in a few years, when the population above, and the trade below, have increased, so that towns, like Cincinnati and Pittsburg, shall be built on convenient landing places. — The finest land in the world, on the banks of the greatest river, with the market at your gate.

The Wabash[1] is 300 yards wide, and rolls its

---

cities, and in 1819, twenty-three. Estwick Evans, in his *Pedestrious Tour* in 1819 writes: "In speaking of large vessels on the Ohio, I may add that ships of large tonnage have been built on this river, laden for the West Indies, and there sold, both vessel and cargo. A person in Europe, unacquainted with the geography of our western waters, would be astonished to see, in the Atlantic Ocean, a large vessel, freighted with country produce, which was built and laden at Pittsburg, between two and three thousand miles from the Gulf of Mexico" (EARLY WESTERN TRAVELS, viii, p. 269). Faux (*Memorable Days*) gives some valuable information (EARLY WESTERN TRAVELS, xi, p. 198). A list of steamboats employed on western rivers between 1812 and 1819 may be found in H. McMurtrie's *Sketches of Louisville and its Environs* (Louisville, 1819), pp. 200-204.

[1] The Wabash, or Ouabache as they called it, was regarded by the French in early times as a very valuable highway between Canada and Louisiana. Croghan, in 1765, wrote that "its course runs through one of the finest countries in the world, the lands being exceedingly rich and well-watered" (EARLY WESTERN TRAVELS, i, p. 137). The river is about 400 miles in length. There is a description of it, almost contemporary with Fordham's, in Lewis C. Beck's *Gazetteer of the States of Illinois and Missouri* (Albany, New York, 1823), pp. 16-17.

warm, transparent, waters over a bed of sand and gravel. It is navigable for keels nine and for batteaux and flats twelve months in the year. It interlocks with the head waters of the Great Miami of the Lakes. Its Eastern fork, the Missisipany, rises in rich low ground, and so near to the springs of St. Mary's, which is the principal branch of the Miami of the lakes, that when the waters are high, boats pass over the intervening land.[1] Congress has voted a piece of land to raise funds for making a Canal here, which will connect the Lakes, the St. Lawrence, and the Northern Ocean with the Mississippi and the Gulf of Mexico. There is some fine land on the Wabash, both above and below St. Vincennes.

Princetown, where we now reside, is situated about ten miles from the Wabash, 12 from the White River, 28 from the Ohio, and 30 South of Vincennes. It stands on a range of hills in the midst of woods. It was laid out 3 years ago, but one cabin stood here 11 years ago. There are three small brick, four or five frame, and seven or eight log, houses, and about a dozen cabins in the town. The stumps of the trees have not yet had time to rot away in the streets, which are therefore dangerous to walk in after dark. We have hired a small frame house, with a log kitchen &c, adjoining a good garden and stable.

---

[1]The sources of the eastern fork of the Wabash and of the St. Mary's are in the vicinity of the present town of Selina, Ohio. By the Miami of the Lakes is meant the Maumee.

The woods around us are inhabited by Indians, bears, wolves, deer, opossums and racoons. We hear the howling of the wolves every evening, as they are driven back from the farmyards by the dogs, who flock together to repel the invaders. In looking in the maps, I find I am wrong in saying, that the Indians inhabit the neighborhood. Their boundary line is thirty miles hence, but they often hunt here.

August 3ᵈ. 11 at night. I delayed finishing this letter, because —— returned two days ago, and M_r. B—— this evening. I am going off tomorrow by sunrise to the Illinois territory, to explore the Little Wabash for a mill seat —— G—— will go part of the way with me.

I am informed that the Illinois is a most beautiful country; — quite unsettled in the interior, with no accommodations for travellers but such as the cabins of the hunter afford. In my next letter I hope I shall be able to give you some important information.

. . . I wish you could see your brother mount his horse to morrow morning. I will give you a sketch. A broad brimmed straw hat, — long trousers and moccasins, — shot pouch and powder horn slung from a belt, — rifle at his back, in a sling, — tomohawk in a holster at his saddle bow, — a pair of saddle bags stuffed with shirts and gingerbread, made by an old friend of yours, — Boat cloak and Scotch tent buckled behind the saddle. . . . Good bye.

P. S. Tell —— and —— that I like them well enough to wish them here. Bears eat neither cows, hogs, nor sheep, till they have been accustomed to see them two or three years; by that time they are hunted away.

VII

Physical character of southern Illinois — The English Prairie — Three lines of communication with the Atlantic — Settlers in and about the English Prairies — Rates of freightage — Cost of travel — A tabular view of products — Fauna of the region — Salt deposits — Cost of building — Advantages of the backwoods settler — Profits of trade — Land the basis of wealth — The Mississippi river system — Slaves and bound persons — Classes of frontier settlers — Character of the backwoodsman — Democratic manners — Signs of progress — How to take up land — Eastern ignorance of the West — The climate — Size of the Illinois Territory — Opportunities for capital in Illinois — No prejudice against liberal-minded Englishmen.

Shawanoe town[1] *Illinois Territory*
Nov[r]. *15. 1817.*

I AM here resting from a journey through part of the Wabash country, and I gladly seize this opportunity of describing it. But I must first ex-

---

[1] Shawneetown, so named because of the identification in early times of the Shawnee Indians with its locality, was laid out in 1808. It is situated in Gallatin County, Illinois, twelve miles north of the junction of the Saline River with the Ohio. Cuming tells us in his *Sketches* that already before the end of 1808 the town comprised twenty-four cabins and was a place of considerable resort on account of the salt-works twelve miles distant [see p. 120, note] (EARLY WESTERN TRAVELS, iv, p. 271). Nuttall, in 1818, called the place a mere "handful of log cabins" (EARLY WESTERN TRAVELS, xiii, p. 71). In the summer of the same year William Tell Harris visited it, afterwards writing in his *Remarks* (p. 139): "From the situation of Shawneetown its inhabitants might be supposed to partake of the nature of the wild duck, for every year they expect to be driven, by the waters, to their upper stories, as land high enough to avoid them is not to be found within a mile of the place; the consequent unhealthiness of such a spot is apparent in the sallow complexions of those who here deprive themselves of many comforts, and risk both health and life, for the sake of gain; considerable business being done here, as it is on the road from the southern States to St. Louis, and the Missouri, and the land-office is here." This land-office was for the southeast district of Illinois and had been established only a few months before Harris wrote. Fearon, in his *Sketches* (p. 260), says the town had still only about thirty log houses when he visited it in 1817. Its chief importance lay in its situation respecting the chief routes of trade, especially down the Ohio and from south central Illinois.

press my regret that I have not yet received a letter from old England. . . .

That part of the Illinois Territory[1] which lies between the great and little Wabash rivers and south of the latter to the Ohio, is about as hilly as Hertfordshire. It is intersected with a vast number of streams or creeks, and interspersed with prairies or natural meadows, containing from 1,000 to 100,000 acres. They are very irregular in figure, and are dotted and clumped with trees, like English parks. Some of the smallest are low, flat, and swampy, but the greatest part are high, dry, and rolling. The soil of the latter is generally light, and very rich; consisting of a due mixture of vegetable mould, sand, and clay lying on sand rock.

[1] The stages in the political evolution of the Illinois Territory may be indicated briefly. December 12, 1778, after the conquest by George Rogers Clark, the legislature of Virginia constituted what was known as the County of Illinois. In 1784 the region was ceded to the nation by Virginia, and it then became a part of the Northwest Territory, definitely organized in 1787. By act of May 7, 1800, Congress divided the Northwest Territory, giving the name Indiana to all west of a line beginning on the Ohio opposite the mouth of the Kentucky River and continuing through Fort Recovery to the northern limits of the United States [see p. 101, note]. As the population of the Illinois country grew, a strong demand was made for a separate territorial organization. The result was that by act of February 23, 1809, the Territory of Illinois was set aside from Indiana, with boundaries the same as those of the present state, except that they extended northward to Canada. Ninian Edwards was appointed first governor, and Kaskaskia was made the capital. [For admission to statehood see p. 174, note 2.] On the early history of Illinois the following works will be found useful: John Reynolds, *The Pioneer History of Illinois* (Chicago, 1887); Henry Brown, *History of Illinois from its first Discovery and Settlement* (New York, 1844); Ninian W. Edwards, *History of Illinois from 1777 to 1783; and Life and Times of Ninian Edwards* (Springfield, 1870); Alexander Davidson and Bernard Stuvé, *Complete History of Illinois from 1673 to 1873* (Springfield, 1874); and John Moses, *Illinois, Historical and Statistical* (Chicago, 1889).

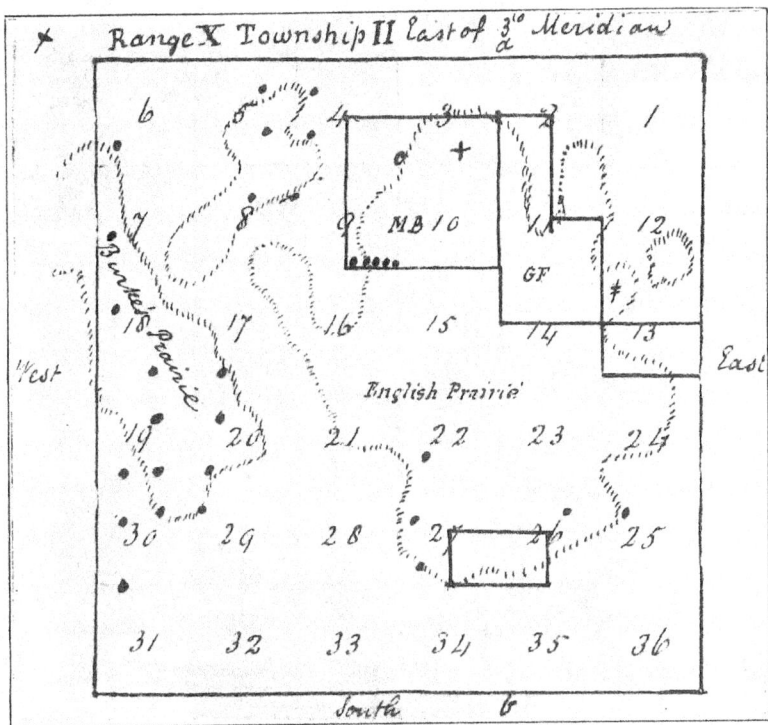

ENGLISH PRAIRIE

Every square is one mile, and contains 640 acres. Thirty-six miles form a township. The squares are called sections and are sold entire or in quarters, price 2$ in four annual installments. Discount for cash 6 p^r cent.

Limestone has been found in the Piankeshaw village prairie,[1] which is divided from the Boltonhouse[2] or English Prairie by only two miles of timbered land. On the English Prairie very excellent brick earth has been found by M[r]. Birkbeck. The English Prairie[3] lies in Latitude 38° 30' North, and Longitude 88° west of London. It is 4½ miles long and 4 miles wide. It is high on the North and East sides and has some beautiful situations for houses. A creek runs through it, and there are a dozen branches which are filled by every shower of rain.

M[r]. Birkbeck's[4] house will be on the spot marked

---

[1] A district west from Vincennes which took its name from the Piankeshaw Indians, a branch of the Miamis, who had inhabited it when it first became known to the whites.

[2] "The English prairie was first called Boltinghouse prairie, from a young man of that name, who was killed by the Indians a few years ago." John Woods, *Two Years' Residence* (EARLY WESTERN TRAVELS, x, p. 270).

[3] For Birkbeck's description of this prairie — the special field of his colonizing operations — see his *Notes*, pp. 129-131. It lay almost due north of the mouth of the Great Wabash, about forty-five miles from its shipping port, Shawneetown.

[4] For facts regarding Birkbeck and his Illinois settlement see Introduction, p. 23 *et seq.* A full account may be found in George Flower's *History of the English Settlement in Edwards County, Illinois* (Chicago, 1882), edited by Elihu B. Washburne, as Volume I of the Chicago Historical Society's *Collections.* Contemporary descriptions of the settlement are Woods, *Two Years' Residence* (EARLY WESTERN TRAVELS, x, p. 271); Welby, *Visit to North America* (EARLY WESTERN TRAVELS, xii, p. 248, ff.); William Tell Harris, *Remarks*, pp. 137-139; and William Faux, *Memorable Days* (EARLY WESTERN TRAVELS, xi, p. 252, ff.). The observations made by these writers, with the exception of Woods, were generally unfavorable. Adam Hodgson, in his *Letters from North America* (London, 1824), ii, pp. 64-77, gives a very discouraging report of the enterprise, based, however, not on personal knowledge, but merely on the complaints of discontented settlers who were returning East from the Illinois country. A fairly useful essay entitled "Morris Birkbeck and his Friends," by Daniel Barry, has appeared in Publication No. 9 of the Illinois State Historical Library (Springfield, 1904), pp. 259-273.

+, and we have a hunting cabin on the spot marked o; and there will probably be a range of cottages on the dotted line ....

The little Wabash,[1] a fine mill stream, which descends from the North 2 or 300 miles, is six miles west of the Prairie. The big Wabash, a navigable river, which interlocks with the Miami of the Lakes, will probably be connected with it by a canal; at present the portage is 8 miles. The Indian traders ascend the Wabash, descend the Miami, and traverse Lake Erie in 30 days. We have thus at our very doors 3 lines of communication with the Atlantic, chiefly, or entirely, by water. 1st. from Baltimore, Pittsburg, and the Ohio. 2d. The Wabash, the Lakes, and the St. Lawrence. 3d. The Wabash, the Ohio, and the Mississippi. On all these rivers there are large commercial towns.

The Steam boats descend the Ohio and the Mississippi so rapidly that I could be with you in Hertfordshire, via New Orleans, in two months.

The spaces on the map contained by the dark lines are Mr. Birkbeck's and Mr. Flower's purchases.[2] They have divided them by a meridian

---

[1] The Little Wabash rises near the source of the Kaskaskia, in central Illinois, flows southward, and empties into the Great Wabash in Gallatin County, Illinois.

[2] For facts regarding the settlement of George Flower and subsequently his father Richard, in Illinois, see Introduction, pp. 23-27. The best account of the whole Birkbeck-Flower enterprise is the younger Flower's *History of the English Settlement in Edwards County, Illinois*, referred to in note 4, p. 115. This book was written during the author's later years, when, after suffering financial reverses, he was living with his children in southern Indiana and Illinois. The unfortunate quarrel which alienated the

line a.b. Besides this, they have made entry of another prairie, near the little Wabash. The dots are entries made by American Back-woodsmen.

All but six have been made since August. There were none at that time in the Village Prairie, two miles to the North of us: there are now 15. A M^r. DePugh made an entry of a quarter section in the Village Prairie; a month afterwards, he wished to sell in order to purchase close to our settlement, and he has been bid 3½$ p^r. acre for his land.

Let us go back to the means of access to our settlement. It is on a ridge between the Great and Little Wabash; nearly equi-distant from both. The former is always navigable; the latter two months in the year; and two days ago, I signed a petition to the Governor, requesting permission and authority to form a Company, for the purpose of rendering it permanently navigable.

M^r. Birkbeck's and Flower's purchase in the Brushy Prairie[1] will then be greatly inhanced in value, — for it lies within two miles of it.

The present rate of freightage is — from Shawnee to Orleans 1$ per hundred lbs. — back 4½$ — to Pittsburg 3½$ — from Pittsburg 1$ — from Louisville, Kentucky, 37½ cents — from Shawnee, or the

Birkbeck and Flower families soon after the settlement was established is related in detail in Faux's *Memorable Days* (EARLY WESTERN TRAVELS, xi, p. 272, ff.).

[1] The Brushy Prairie lay on the east bank of the Little Wabash (in Wayne County), seven miles southwest of Albion and eleven east of Fairfield.

mouth of the Wabash, to Carmi,[1] on the little Wabash, 20 miles below us, 37½ cents — to the nearest point of the Wabash to our settlement 50 cents — down the stream to Shawnee 5 cents p[r]. hundred lbs — from Vincennes on the Wabash to the Boon pas [2] — 5 cents.

Passage in Stage and expenses of a journey from Philadelphia to Pittsburg 50$ — Journey down the Ohio 900 miles 10 to 15$ — To Orleans 30$ by Steamboat and back again up the Mississippi 90$ — To St. Louis, by the Steamboat, 20$ — by land on horseback 8$.

The Illinois territory produces the finest crops of corn and grain of any country in the world.

I will give you a rough estimate of produce per acre and value.[3]

			$ Cents	
Indian Corn — 50 to 80 bushels	.	.	.25	per bush.
Wheat — 25 to 30	. . .	.	.75	
Barley — say 32	. .	.	.75	
Oats — 50	. . .	.	.37½	
Tobacco — 12 to 15 hundred lbs.	.	.	4.50	per hundred lbs.
Cotton for domestic manufacture	.	.	40.00	
Pork — fatted in the woods	.	.	3.50	
Do. — corn-fed	. . .	.	4.00	

[1] Carmi, seat of White County, Illinois, is twenty miles above the mouth of the Little Wabash.

[2] The Bonpas is a small stream to the east of the English Prairie, flowing southward and emptying into the Great Wabash about forty-five miles below Vincennes. It forms the present eastern boundary of Edwards County. On the creek, twelve miles distant from Albion, was a little village known as Bonpas which served as a "port" for the English settlement. Commodities were carried back and forth between the settlement and this station on horses or in wagons. The waterway from Bonpas to Shawneetown was about sixty miles in length.

[3] A table of prices, wages, etc. in Kentucky at about the same time is given by Flint in his *Letters from America* (EARLY WESTERN TRAVELS, ix, pp. 139-140); one for Ohio may be found in Hulme's *Journal* (EARLY WESTERN TRAVELS, x, pp. 74-75).

Beef	5.00
Hides	12.00 pr. hundd. lbs.
Maple Sugar	37.50 ——
Honey	.75 per gallon.
A day's work	.50 with board.
A labourer's board	.12½
A horse and man, one day . . .	1.00 } without board.
Do. with a plough . . .	1.25 }
A good horse	60.00
A handsome saddle horse . .	100.00
A Cow	20.00
An Ox	12.00
A Sow with Pigs	6.00

Shop-goods — double what they are in England.

In the Woods there are great quantities of Grapes, Walnuts, Hickory Nuts, and Parsimins; and, in low river bottoms, Pocoons, a species of thin shelled walnut, and little pappaws. Raspberries and strawberries grow wild; as do also hops and indigo. Hemp and flax are cultivated; and I have eaten in these wilds as fine musk and water Melons, as I have in France.[1]

Game is as plentiful here as in other parts of the U. S. east of the Mississippi. Bears, Deer, Racoons, and Beavers, are chiefly valued by the hunters. There are wolves, a very few panthers, and some elk in remote situations; Also Turkeys, Pheasants, American Partridges, prairie Hens, and innumerable Squirrels, which are delicious food. The rivers abound with fish, some species of which weigh upwards of 100 lbs.[2]

There are many Salt ponds. Those at the Saline

---

[1] A full description of the plant life of the Illinois prairies is given in Woods, *Two Years' Residence* (EARLY WESTERN TRAVELS, x, pp. 292-309).

[2] The fauna of the Illinois country is described by Woods, *Two Years' Residence* (EARLY WESTERN TRAVELS, x, pp. 281-292).

8

river near Shawnee, yield 150,000 bushels of salt annually at 75 Cents per bushel. The Wabash, White River, Ohio, and Illinois rivers have coal banks. I cannot enumerate all the natural productions of this fine country, which literally flows with milk and honey. "Man is the only growth that's wanted here:" and that want will soon be supplied. Every log Cabin is swarming with half-naked children. Boys of 18 build huts, marry, and raise hogs and children at about the same expence.

A Cabin of rough logs, containing 2 rooms costs 50$ — Ditto, smoothed by the axe 60$. A brick house containing 4 rooms 12 feet square with shingled roof 600$. A Kitchen detached, log built 30$. Smoke house 20$. Stable for 4 horses, with loft, 35$. Corn house 30$. Barn 100$. Fencing with split-rails 25 Cents per rod. Ditching in the Prairies 31¼; one rail and stakes to do, with hedge planted, perhaps, 12½ Cents more.

Farming will not, perhaps, pay more per Cent here than it does in England, if the farmers personal labour be deducted. There is an obvious reason for this; although we are here 1500 miles from the sea, yet the water communication is so expeditious and cheap, that the prices in West Indian and

---

[1] The salt-works on the Saline were about twelve miles from Shawneetown. They supplied the settlers of all southern Illinois and a large portion of those in Indiana, Ohio, Kentucky, and in the territories along the lower Mississippi. Woods tells us that by 1820 they produced about 300,000 bushels annually. Prior to 1818 the salt-works were held as a government reservation, the surrounding land being leased to the operators. When Illinois was admitted to the Union the proprietorship of the salt fields was given over to the new commonwealth.

European Markets affect the value of produce here, so wonderfully and beautifully does the commerce undisturbed by war connect men living in the most distant regions, and equalize the profits of producing food.

But, still the advantage is greatly in favour of the back settler in America: His table is profusely furnished; if he choose, with delicacies: He is lord of the soil he cultivates: His land tax, on first rate land, is 1 Cent per acre; on second rate ¾ of a Cent: And the lowest estimate of the annual rise of the value of his Estate, even when unimproved by cultivation and building, is 16 per Cent per annum on first cost.

Trade, from the general want of capital, and other causes with which I am unacquainted, is exceedingly profitable. 75 to 100 per Cent is reckoned a good profit; 50 per cent is a living profit; 25 p^r. cent, will not keep a man to his business, he will look out for something else. A Tanner is now in the room, who has quitted N. York and a business which paid him 30 p^r. Cent. He is going to St. Louis to establish himself there with the expectation of getting Cent per Cent.

I had the following account from a River Trader

	Dr.		Cr.
A boat of 36 tons burden from Orleans to Louisville	$		$
14 men at 75$ . . .	1050	Freight of 36 tons at 90$	3240
—board for 75 days .	525	Deduct expences . . .	1750
—extra pay to Steersman	75		
—wear of boat . . .	100	Clear profit remaining .	1490
	1750		

Freighting down to Orleans will pay the expence of going, and leave one or two hundred dollars overplus. But if, besides 700 dollars, the price of a new boat completely rigged, the owner has a capital of 1500 or 2000$, he may make the Voyage down pay him from 500 to 1500 dollars. The whole trip is completed in two or three months. Steam boats pay better interest still, and are gradually increasing in number and perfection of machinery. . . .

Moreover, LAND is the basis of wealth. The possession of it is sure to enrich the purchaser, if he has selected it with any judgment. The enhancement of its value does not depend on contingent circumstances, but on the never ceasing and progressive increase of the human race. We are here on the most favorable spot for buying it; we have headed the tide of Emigration.

My friends have made their election almost before a civilized being had set his foot upon this ground, which a few months ago was traversed only by the Savage or the hunter. From the contemplation of an entire continent, they descended to the examination of limited states. With minds unbiassed and intensely fixed upon its object they have passed by every district that offered peculiar advantages, till they found one that contained an aggregate of all: — the climate of Virginia, — the fertility of Ohio, — a commercial communication with the Ocean, — Prairies, like those of the Missouri, — the Minerals from the North and East, — and — freedom from slavery.

If you will look at any of the Maps constructed since the Travels of Pike or Lewis and Clarke have been published,[1] and the surveys of the Land Offices have been exhibited, you will see that Rivers, to which the Thames is but an insignificant stream, are from the North, the East, and the West, into the Valley of the Mississippi, "the father of waters." This again rolls the floods of half a Continent into

---

[1] The western explorations of Zebulon Pike and of Meriwether Lewis and William Clark, between 1804 and 1807, had their origin in the desire of President Jefferson to find out what sort of country it was that, under the name of Louisiana, had recently been purchased from Napoleon. Pike made two exploring trips of importance. The first was undertaken in 1805, under the immediate direction of General James Wilkinson. It comprised an ascent of the Mississippi from St. Louis for the purpose of selecting sites for military posts, treating with the northern Indians, and ascertaining whether the British were in possession of any places on the Canadian frontier properly belonging to the United States. Cass Lake, at the mouth of Turtle River, was the limit of this expedition. The second trip was longer and more important. It was undertaken in 1806 and embraced an ascent of the Missouri as far as the Osage, an overland passage through Kansas to the Arkansas, an ascent of this river as far as Leadville, Colorado, and a capture in 1807 by Spanish dragoons on the Rio Grande del Norte, which afforded an unexpected opportunity to view the lands and peoples of the Southwest. The first record of Pike's travels given to the public was *An Account of Expeditions to the Sources of the Mississippi, and through the Western Parts of Louisiana, to the Sources of the Arkansaw*, etc. (Philadelphia, 1810). The book went through numerous editions. The best for use to-day is Elliott Coues (editor), *The Expeditions of Zebulon Montgomery Pike to the Headwaters of the Mississippi River, through Louisiana Territory, and in New Spain, during the Years 1805-6-7* (New York, 1895). It appears that Jefferson planned some such expedition as that later undertaken by Lewis and Clark while the Louisiana territory was still a French possession and in the hands of the Spaniards. After June, 1803, when the news of the purchase treaty reached America, preparations which had been begun under cover were rapidly pushed to completion. Captain Lewis, a Virginian and the President's private secretary, was designated to head the enterprise, and by him another Virginian, Captain Clark, was selected as chief associate. The Lewis and Clark party, twenty-nine in num-

a Gulf, which seems to be designed by Nature to be the very focus of Commerce — the centre of the habitable world. The Illinois territory is watered by five of the most important of these streams. It is bounded by no tract of land intended by Nature to be a desert. Northward lies one inland Sea, and North Eastward, it has water communication with another. The ease with which property is acquired by the industrious, produces an equality unknown in old Countries. No white man or woman will bear being called a servant, but they will gladly do your work.

ber, spent the winter of 1803-04 in camp at the mouth of the Missouri; the summer and autumn of 1804 in ascending the Missouri; the winter of 1804-05 in a stockade among the Mandan Indians in North Dakota; the summer and autumn of 1805 in pushing on across the mountains to the Pacific coast; the winter of 1805-06 in camp at Fort Clatsop, studying the country and its resources; and the summer of 1806 in effecting the return journey to St. Louis. The explorers, according to instructions, kept elaborate journals, and in 1807 one of these — that of Patrick Gass — was published. In the same year a Philadelphia house put out a prospectus announcing the forthcoming publication of the journals kept by Lewis and Clark. Lewis, however, was soon made governor of the Louisiana Territory and Clark was appointed superintendent of Indian Affairs and brigadier-general of militia — positions which involved heavy duties and seriously delayed the preparation of the journals for the press. In 1809 Lewis took up the work afresh, but met his death before getting well started. Clark then secured the assistance of an editor in the person of Nicholas Biddle of Philadelphia and the manuscript was finally prepared — only to be rejected as a publishing venture by every one to whom submitted until 1813. The work was finally seen through the press by a Philadelphia newspaper man by the name of Paul Allen. The Biddle-Allen edition of the journals was a mere paraphrase, made as readable as possible by the omission of practically all of the scientific data, which in fact gave the writings their chief claim to value. Fortunately the original manuscripts were secured by Jefferson, being placed for safe keeping in the archives of the American Philosophical Society. Due to the enterprise of this organization we have now a most excellent reprint of the journals, edited by Dr. R. G. Thwaites under the title *Original Journals of the Lewis and Clark Expedition, 1804-1806* (New York, 1904), 7 volumes and Atlas.

Your hirelings must be spoken to with Civility and cheerfulness. Domestic services, perhaps, will be obtained with difficulty.

Respectable families from Kentucky, who do not distinguish between a Servant and a Slave, do all their domestic work, except washing, with their own hands; others indenture negroes for 10 or 15 years; but having been accustomed to treat their Slaves with severity, they generally spoil the tempers of their bound servants, whom they have not so much under command.

The people who live on these frontiers may be divided into four classes, — not perfectly distinct yet easily distinguishable.[1]

1st. The hunters, a daring, hardy, race of men, who live in miserable cabins, which they fortify in times of War with the Indians, whom they hate but much resemble in dress and manners. They are unpolished, but hospitable, kind to Strangers, honest and trustworthy. They raise a little Indian corn, pumpkins, hogs, and sometimes have a Cow

---

[1] Fearon, in his *Sketches of America* (pp. 263-264) says: "The inhabitants of Illinois may, perhaps, be ranked as follows: First, the Indian hunters, who are neither different in character or pursuits from their ancestors in the days of Columbus. 2nd, The 'Squatters,' who are half-civilized and half-savage. These are, in character and habits, extremely wretched: indeed, I prefer the genuine *uncontaminated* Indian. 3rd, A medley of land jobbers, lawyers, doctors, and farmers, who traverse this immense continent, founding settlements, and engaging in all kinds of speculation. 4th, Some old French settlers, possessed of considerable property, and living in ease and comfort." Another attempt to classify the population of the West will be found in Flint's *Letters* (EARLY WESTERN TRAVELS, ix, pp. 232-236). Cuming, *Sketches* (EARLY WESTERN TRAVELS, iv, pp. 135-140) and Bradbury, *Travels* (EARLY WESTERN TRAVELS, v, pp. 281-287) have descriptions of value for a somewhat earlier period.

or two, and two or three horses belonging to each family: But their rifle is their principal means of support. They are the best marksmen in the world, and such is their dexterity that they will shoot an apple off the head of a companion. Some few use the bow and arrow. I have spent 7 or 8 weeks with these men, have had opportunities of trying them, and believe they would sooner give me the last shirt off their backs, than rob me of a charge of powder. Their wars with the Indians have made them vindictive. This class cannot be called first Settlers, for they move every year or two.

2^d. class. First settlers;—a mixed set of hunters and farmers. They possess more property and comforts than the first class; yet they are a half barbarous race. They follow the range pretty much; selling out when the Country begins to be well settled, and their cattle cannot be entirely kept in the woods.

3^d. class. —is composed of enterprising men from Kentucky and the Atlantic States. This class consists of Young Doctors, Lawyers, Storekeepers, farmers, mechanics &c, who found towns, trade, speculate in land, and begin the fabric of Society. There is in this class every *gradation* of *intellectual* and *moral* character; but the general tone of Social manners is yet too much relaxed. There is too much reliance upon personal prowess, and the laws have not yet acquired sufficient energy to prevent violence.

Such are the Inhabitants of the Southern parts of

Indiana, and of Shawanoe town, St. Louis, St. Geneviève,[1] and the large settlements on the Mississippi.

4th. class—old settlers, rich, independent, farmers, wealthy merchants, possessing a good deal of
information, a knowledge of the world, and an
enterprising spirit. Such are the Ohio men, Western Pennsylvanians, Kentuckians and Tenessee
men. The young men have a military taste, and
most of them have served in the late war. They
were great duellists, but now the laws against duelling are more strictly enforced; they carry dirks,
and sometimes decide a dispute on the spot. Irritable and dissipated in youth, yet they are generally steady and active in Manhood. They undertake with facility, and carry on with unconquerable
ardour, any business or speculation that promises
great profit, and sustain the greatest losses with a
firmness that resembles indifference.

You will perceive from this slight sketch, which
I have made as impartially as I am able, that the
Backwoods men, as they are called somewhat contemptuously by the Inhabitants of the Atlantic
States, are admirably adapted by Nature and education for the scenes they live and act in. The
prominent feature of their character is power. The
young value themselves on their courage, the old

---

[1] The original Ste. Geneviève was situated about three miles south
of the present town of the name, in Ste. Geneviève County, Missouri.
The date of its founding is uncertain; 1732 is not improbable.
In 1763, when the Louisiana territory east of the Mississippi was
transferred by France to England, Ste. Geneviève, being one of the
two French towns on the western bank of the Mississippi, received
a considerable influx of population from the ceded country. But
it never became a place of importance.

on their shrewdness. The veriest villains have something grand about them. They expect no mercy and they shew no fear; "every man's hand is against them, and their hand is against every man's."

As social Comforts are less under the protection of the laws here, than in old countries, friendship and good neighbourhood are more valued. A man of good character is an acquisition; not that there is a small proportion of such men, but because the bad are as undisguisedly bad, as their opposites are professedly good. This is not the land of Hypocrisy. It would not here have its reward. Religion is not the road to worldly respectability, nor a possession of it the cloak to immorality.

I wish I could give you a correct idea of the perfect equality that exists among these republicans. A Judge leaves the Court house, shakes hands with his fellow citizens and retires to his loghouse. The next day you will find him holding his own plough. The Lawyer has the title of Captain, and serves in his Military capacity under his neighbour, who is a farmer and a Colonel. The shop keeper sells a yard of tape, and sends shiploads of produce to Orleans; he travels 2000 miles in a year; he is a good hunter, and has been a soldier; he dresses and talks as well as a London Merchant, and probably has a more extensive range of ideas; at least he has fewer prejudices. One prejudice, however, nothing will induce him to give up — he thinks the Americans in general, and particularly those of his own state, are the best soldiers in the world. Such is the native Shopkeeper: the Eastern Emigrant is very different.

I have not seen an effeminate, or a feeble man, in mind or body, belonging to these Western Countries. The most ignorant, compared with men of the same standing in England, are well informed. Their manners are coarse; but they have amongst themselves a code of politeness, which they generally observe. Drinking whisky is the greatest pest, the most fertile source of disorders, amongst them. When intoxicated by it, they sometimes fight most furiously. In this they resemble the Lower Irish.

There is an universal spirit of enquiry amongst all classes of people. In the state of Indiana, in which there is but one town that is of six years standing, there are several Book-clubs. Newspapers and Reviews from Philadelphia, Baltimore, Kentucky, and S^t. Louis, are received weekly. When we arrived at Princetown, there was no Post-office nearer than Vincennes; now we have the Mail once a fortnight, and shall soon have a Western and a Southern mail every week.

M^r. Birkbeck was known here by his writings, before he came to America. His tour through France has been read at S^t. Louis.[1] His settlement

---

[1] George Flower, in his *History of the English Settlement in Edwards County, Illinois* (p. 23), tells of the writing of this book as follows: "After the downfall of Napoleon the First, and the peace succeeding to a twenty-years' war, Mr. Birkbeck invited me to accompany him in a journey to France, to which I readily acceded. We travelled together three months in that country, avoiding the usual route of English travel. Passing from north to south, to the shores of the Mediterranean, skirting the Pyrenees, and re-

has already attracted the attention of Land Speculators and Farmers. W—— of Philadelphia writes: "I have directed 120 Germans to you; they are proceeding toward Ohio, and you will probably receive a deputation from them."

M^r. J—— of Philadelphia wishes to send a number of families to our neighbourhood. I met him at Cincinnati in September. He requested me to select 5,000 acres for him; which I declined to do. He wants 20,000 acres.

I think of entering some land about Sections 12 and 13. The land is high, soil light, and tolerably rich. Timber — good; not standing thick, but pretty large; it is black oak, hickory, walnut, with some white oak. A Stream winds through a narrow valley between the hills, and the house if placed on the mark # would command a view of the whole prairie, and have a southern and western aspect.

If any persons in England would like to possess a small stake in this Country, I could procure it for them thus. A.B. in England advances the first and second installments of ½$ per acre per annum. I pay the third and fourth, and have the option of holding the land as a partner, or of selling it by auction. If I should fail in making my payments, the land is secured to us for five years. It would

turning through the heart of the country by a more easterly route to Paris, we saw more of the country and Frenchmen at home, than we otherwise should, if confined to any one of the popular routes of travel. . . . On our return Mr. Birkbeck published his 'Notes of a Journey through France' [London: W. Phillips, 1814]. It had a wide circulation in England, and was well known in America. It was the first book I met with at Monticello, the residence of Thomas Jefferson."

then be sold by the U. S. and the overplus of 2$ would revert to the original purchasers. To a share of this overplus I should then relinquish all claim, and return it entire to my partner A.B. But, if ♦I pay my installments, I should be an equal sharer with A.B., putting my knowledge of land acquired by travelling, and studying the subject on the spot, and also my trouble, against the credit of 1 dollar per acre for two years. This is the plan M^r. E—— acts upon.

Were you to ask me, "Do you think the Illinois Territory would be the best place in the U. S. for me to emigrate to, supposing that I could with propriety and prudence leave England?" I should hesitate in giving an affirmative to this question. You want the society that is to be found near old established towns, comforts ready made to your hands. You ought to enjoy them at your time of life. Easy and constant intercourse with Europe, a quiet and respectable neighbourhood, religious institutions, and access to large libraries, are advantages you would probably not like to forego. The vicinity of Philadelphia, the Jerseys, many parts of the State of New York, present them all to you.

The inhabitants of the Eastern ports know no more about this country, than you do in England. Some are afraid to cross the Mountains: so many terrible stories of it are in circulation. Kentucky, or Bloody Ground, as it used to be called, seems to them to be the verge of the habitable world. These prejudices are, however, disappearing. The rising, and already important, commerce of the West is becoming an object of their jealousy. The poorer and more enterprising of the farmers leave the inhospitable climates of the North, and find here fertile lands and short winters.

The hottest weather of July and August did not injure my health; yet the thermometer was frequently as high as 90, generally at 80 at noon. I enjoyed that weather very much. This Autumn more rain has fallen than has ever been remembered at this season of the year. It has at length ceased, and we have now fine sunshiny days and slightly frosty nights. Heavy freezing, I am told, sets in at Christmas, and lasts from three to six weeks. Then the snow melts, and Spring comes on rapidly. I have been writing all day with the door open to the road, and this is the 24th. day of November.

Farmers are now gathering their Indian corn, which they pick from the stalks. Their wheat was cut in June, and housed in July. They will begin soon to kill their pork for the Orleans market.

I have written a long letter of heterogeneous observations just as they have arisen in my mind. You will perceive that I have taken care to state every thing exactly as the impressions I have felt were left upon me. So rapid is improvement in this Country, that by the time you read them, circumstances will be altered, and many statements will be incorrect.

I must add a word or two more. The Illinois

Territory has but a small proportion of Indian Lands. In this it has greatly the advantage of Indiana, in which state the Indians possess two thirds of the soil.[1] So that, in the improbable event of another war, there will be no fighting near the English settlement. We shall of course be called upon, and be ready, I hope, to defend our neighbours; for here every man is a soldier.

Illinois is 300 miles long and 200 broad; it contains 50,000 square miles, or 32 millions of acres. It is supposed to contain 30,000 inhabitants, who are scattered about, chiefly on the banks of rivers.

There is so much to be done and such a field for exertion, that no one need be discouraged from

---

[1] The lands comprising the present state of Indiana were acquired from the Indians by means of a long series of treaties and agreements between 1795 and 1840. By the treaty of Greenville, negotiated by General Wayne in 1795, the work was begun by the acquisition of large tracts, mainly in Ohio, but including lands in the future Indiana Territory on the Wabash and at the junction of the St. Mary and St. Joseph, and George Rogers Clark's grant on the Ohio. When, in 1800, William Henry Harrison was made governor of the newly organized Territory, he was invested with general powers to conclude treaties with the natives relating to the proprietorship of lands. In this work he was active and successful. By five successive treaties, between 1802 and 1805, he acquired for the United States a title to all the Indian lands along the Ohio River, from the mouth of the Wabash to the western boundary of the state of Ohio. In 1809, by the treaty of Fort Wayne, he secured the cession of about 3,000,000 acres on the Wabash in the region of present Parke County, though Tecumseh and his brother, the Prophet, refused to recognize the new arrangement. This was the status when Fordham wrote, in 1817. Thereafter a prolonged series of cessions was arranged, until in 1840 the last Indian title to extensive lands within the bounds of the state was extinguished. By most of the final treaties small " reservations " were set aside, but these have now generally passed out of Indian possession. A few descendants of the Miamis still live in Wabash and Miami counties. For an elaborate account of the Indian cessions of land in Indiana, with an excellent map illustrating the subject, see William Henry Smith, *History of the State of Indiana* (Indianapolis, 1897), i, pp. 221-239.

coming here, by the fear of wanting Markets for produce, or for his labour. A capital of £50,000 could be as easily employed here as in England, and with great advantage to the country and to the capitalist. This is not a random guess: I could prove it, and calculate results. A man may fall into poverty here, as well as elsewhere; but the proportion of those who succeed is greater here, than in any place I have ever been in. Every thing and every body is in motion: no standing still, and living upon interest of capital: but every man has his business or employment. . . .

P. S. Rough and democratic as these backwoodsmen are, they shew great respect to talent, to superior knowledge, to age, and to wealth. There is no danger to an European who possesses these advantages, of being jostled, or of not being of consequence among his neighbours. The respect that is shewn to M[r]. B. is even more marked than that he commanded in England from his labourers. Lord Selkirk[1] and suite were at Vincennes the other

---

[1] Thomas Dundas, fifth earl of Selkirk, was born in Kirkcudbrightshire, Scotland, in 1771. He was educated at the University of Edinburgh and in 1799 succeeded to the title and property of his father. His life was devoted largely to the promotion of emigration to British America. As early as 1802 he put forth considerable effort to influence the British Government to provide for the transportation of discontented and impoverished Scottish peasants to the New World. In 1811 he secured from the Hudson Bay Company a large tract of fertile land in the valleys of the Assiniboin and Red River of the North, where, late in the same year, his first band of colonists was established. Many difficulties were encountered, arising chiefly from the opposition of the Northwest traders to the enterprise, and in 1816-17 the settlement was broken up. It was soon restored, however, under Selkirk's personal supervision, and the conflict was transferred to the courts, where the energetic promoter at length secured judgment in favor of his

day at a dinner and ball, and received the most marked attentions. But worth and talent, without Rank, will command respect. Indeed, no rank is known here, but military rank, and that is obtained by tavern-keepers and farmers.

English Aristocrats could not live here. But such men as you would be judges, Magistrates, and respected Citizens.

---

avowed rights. In 1816 Selkirk published *A Sketch of the British Fur Trade*, and in the next year *The Red River Settlement*. He died in 1820.

VIII

A trip down the Patoka — Winter labors and amusements — Christmas — Legislation against duelling — A journey to Cincinnati — Lack of scenery — Difficulties of travel — A frontier judge — Fredericksburg — Albany — Louisville — Shelbyville — Cost of lodgings — Frankfort — The Kentuckians — Arrival at Cincinnati.

Princeton, Indiana. Decr. 7, 1817. As it will be agreeable to myself, and, perhaps, amusing to my relations in England, to review the occurrences and difficulties of settling the Bolton-house, or English, Prairie, and as I shall have an opportunity of seeing *ab initio* an English settlement in the wilderness of the Illinois, I will keep a record of our transactions.

The prairie is fine, dry, light land, and rolling. It contains about 16 square miles, and lies about 6 miles from each of the Wabashes. The country around is healthy, although at a distance there are swampy places.

A few weeks ago, two carpenters (and the wife of one of them) arrived uninvited from England.

Yesterday I purchased a batteau on Mill Pond, for 3$ and Isaac P—— repaired it.

This morning I sent Isaac to Harmony on horseback to buy saws, with directions to proceed across the Wabash to Carmi; there to get provisions and necessaries, which he is to get hauled to the English Prairie.

Jacob P—— and his wife, B——d B., and myself are going down the Patoka[1] in the batteau, for the

---

[1] The Patoka is a small stream flowing westward through Dubois, Pike, and Gibson counties, Indiana, and emptying into the Great

swamp between this town and Coffee Island[1] has been rendered impassable by the late unprecedented rains. For a week past we have had hard frost; the Thermometer nightly down to 18°. and even to 12°.; to-day, fine balmy weather like the Indian summer. We shall take with us blankets and provisions, as we shall probably have to encamp on the unsettled banks of the Patoka.

Monday Decr. 7th.—Put the batteau on the carriage of a waggon, and sent it off to the Patoka with J. P——, who is directed to make oars &c, and to launch the boat. Yesterday 8 men on foot armed with pistols and rifles came into the town from Harmony. They had been in pursuit of an absconded debtor from Vincennes.

Decr. 8th. B——d, P——'s wife, and myself went on horseback to T——'s on the Patoka, where we breakfasted. Loaded the batteau; which was found to be much too small to carry us, our tools, and the various "impedimenta" which were stowed in it. Besides being too small, it was weak and very leaky. We borrowed a canoe in exchange for the skiff; but that was so ticklish that we did not like to venture in it heavily loaded. At last we determined to take both batteau and canoe.

The Patoka crosses Indiana from East to West. It is a deep, but narrow stream, and exceedingly crooked throughout its whole course. Its length

---

Wabash at Mt. Carmel, Illinois. There is a brief description of the valley of the Patoka in William Tell Harris's *Remarks*, p. 133.

[1] Coffee Island is located in the Great Wabash a small distance below Mt. Carmel.

in a right line is about 200 miles. Where we embarked it was about 20 yards wide.

We have been much impeded by fallen trees, some of which lie quite across the river; one we have been obliged to cut through.

I hunted for an hour without success; missed some ducks, my gun being loaded with Buck shot. B——d took his turn. He saw a large herd of deer, but killed nothing but a parroquet.[1]

Encamped at night on the Northern shore. Soil, rich. Timber, — Poplar, Sycamore, Hickory, & Spice. Weather warm, but squally.

Made 15 miles this day.

Decr. 9th. Morning rainy. Caulked the batteau. Weather cleared at 9. Launched our craft. We had not started an hour, before we had a thunder storm and hard rain.

This day the trees were more across the river than yesterday. Nearly lost the batteau on a rapid, which was incumbered by fallen trees. I leaped out with an axe and cut through some branches, and we passed under the trunks. The canoe soon after got again entangled under a fallen tree. Currents very rapid. The axe was employed all day.

Towards evening I left P—— and B——d to dig a channel for the boats round the butt end of

---

[1] Paroquets (a variety of small parrot), which according to reports of travelers were abundant in the Ohio Valley a hundred years ago, are now found only in latitudes much further south. Cuming, in 1807, writing from the mouth of the Scioto, says: " We observed here vast numbers of beautiful, large, green paroquets, which our landlord, squire Brown, informed us abound all over the country. They keep in flocks, and when they alight on a tree, they are not distinguishable from the foliage, from their colour " (EARLY WESTERN TRAVELS, iv, p. 161).

a fallen tree; and I walked across a neck of land to find a camping ground. Had great difficulty in lighting a fire; the wood was so wet.

The Timber and soil nearly the same as yesterday.

— Pappaws and Cane —

The stream was so crooked, that we went towards every point of the compass, and only once had a view down it of 300 yards.

The meal and bread got wet. We shall be on short allowance in two days. Mem^m.—To get a tobacco pouch, with a compartment for matches; for not being able to get logwod bark, I burnt almost all my tow in kindling a fire. Advanced 18 miles.

Decr. 10th. Morning rainy. Waited till nine and started in a drizzling shower, which soon increased to a heavy rain, which lasted all day. Arrived at Coffee Island at night thoroughly soaked.

The banks of the Patoka clayey, and covered generally with cane. The Timber — Hickory, the soil — thin.

The banks of the Wabash low and swampy. The Sycamore is the most common tree on the shore, which spreads its white crooked arms over the stream. The Wabash at Coffee Island is 1,100 yards wide.

Advanced to-day, down the Patoka 15 miles

———————— down the Wabash 9 ——

24.

Slept at M——'s house.

Decr. 11th. We were discouraged from proceeding further by water, and enquired for waggons. There were but two wheeled carriages in the settlement; one was broken and the other rotten. After some delay we engaged a Frenchman to take our plunder[1] on a two horse sleigh, and packed the bedding on a horse, — on which the woman rode. We got to the Boonpas an hour before sun-set. Carried the plunder and the sleigh across in a canoe, and swam the horses. We should have staid, but the Boonpas was rising so fast, — 6 feet in 24 hours, — that we were afraid that the creek at the Deer's lick would be banked up. As it was, we were just in time to cross without difficulty.

In crossing the Cypress creek,[2] before we reached the Boonpas, the bedding got wet. The prairies were half leg deep in water.

No rain to-day, but the weather rather cold. The snow is now drifting into the camp, which we have pitched one mile beyond the crossing.

DuG—— is a complete hunter and an entertaining companion.

Marched to-day 10 miles.

Decr. 13th. *Saturday.* Breakfasted before sunrise and struck our camp. The long prairie is an entire swamp. Waded through several creeks. At 9 a. m. it began to snow, and continued all day.

---

[1] A frontier provincialism for "baggage."

[2] Cypress Creek is a sluggish stream in Gallatin County, Illinois, between Equality and Shawneetown. It flows southward into the Saline River.

At 10 entered our own prairie, and met Isaac P. with the waggon. The water was running rapidly off through the creeks, which were nearly full. Passing the second, the waggon was stuck in the mud, and the sprig tailed mare, upon which B——d and J. P—— were crossing, fell with them into the water.

I left the baggage, and went on to light a fire in the cabin,[1] which we all reached in safety at ½ past 12., though most frozen.

Spent the afternoon in fixing ourselves as well as we could in our cabin.

DuG—— and the waggons left us to return to their respective homes.

The snow is now (9 p. m.) 5 inches deep. We shall sleep in our blankets on Clapboards with our feet to the fire.

Decr. 14th. Sunday. Sent the two P——s to W——'s, about three miles off for the Yager Rifle, and the Wallet, containing my blanket and plunder, and the spade.

We have now a complete set of Sawyer's and Carpenter's tools. B——d went to E——'s and brought back a kettle of honey.

While the men were gone, W—— and another man, who had heard of our arrival, came to call on us. W—— promises to come tomorrow to begin

---

[1] This I had built 2 months ago of round logs, chunked and mudded. It had nothing but the bare earth for the floor at this time, and that trod to mud directly.—FORDHAM.

the other cabin. I hear that another English Emigrant has arrived at Princeton, and is coming out to us with his family.

I searched for a good place to make a saw pit. Made a tent in the house to keep off the snow, which drifts through the roof. Snow to-day a foot deep.

P—— unpacked his base viol and has played several psalm tunes and the evening hymn—the latter recalled England to my mind.

Decr. 15th. The P——'s are making a sawpit. B——d went on the mare to A—— and W——, and bought a hog weighing 200 lbs for 7$. I went surveying. The weather very cold—the snow 14 inches deep.

The soil where the sawpit is dug is rich mould, but thin: next to it lies a hazle mould: beneath lies a fine grey clay, mixed with ochry substances.

Decr. 16th. The P——'s still preparing for sawing. E—— called to ask me to follow a bear, whose track, freshly made, was within 200 yards of our cabin. As I could not go, he returned home.

A—— came with W—— and agreed to build two cabins 12 feet by 14 inside,—standing 16 feet apart, and the roof to be continued over the intermediate space; they are to be chunked, doors to be cut out; joists and sleepers laid: the whole for 25$.

Went with B——d to get a grape vine as a substitute for a chain. After dinner surveyed till dark.

The weather is more mild to-day—some snow, but a Southwest wind has driven away all the clouds. The night is calm and beautiful.

I found to-day a beautiful prisimon tree, about fifty feet high, and a great quantity of fruit upon it, — which are now delicious. They taste like raisins dipped in honey. I have kept some seeds to send to M——.

Dec͏ʳ. 17ᵗʰ. Wednesday. Surveying. Saw some prairie hawks, blue bodies, ash coloured belly and wings, tipped with black.

Came home over the middle creek, into which I fell through the Ice.

Dec͏ʳ. 18ᵗʰ. Bought a deer of B—— for $1.50. He promises to bring in some Turkeys.

W—— brought in a hog, which A—— shot for us.

I planted about a peck of peach stones. Bid W—— good bye.

The settlers are all glad we are going to have a mill built; they have now to pack their meal 25 miles. A—— has been pounding corn for us, and it makes good bread.

Weather still very cold — 7 degrees below zero. . . .

I rather dread my voyage up the Patoka, as we shall have logs, and, perhaps, ice to impede us. S—— has told me how to rig the canoe to the best advantage.

Sawing goes on very slowly: the tools are all new; and the black oak very hard. Every body says that the mill will be carried away by the first hurricane. But, as Smeaton has erected a tower, which withstands the *winds* and *waves* of the Ocean, there is certainly a possibility, that another may be made to stand fast against *wind* alone.[1] It will be the first wind-mill built on this side of the Ohio.

The P——s have been a little disheartened by the difficulty of getting provisions, but now that they have 300 lbs of meat hanging against the wall, they are quite chearful.

B——d and I cut off two ribs from the Buck, spitted them on a sharp pointed stick, and roasted them for our dinner; they were delicious.

Walked to W——s and slept there. We could not take our pack horse across the Boonpas, because of the Ice. We were therefore obliged to leave him tied to a tree, with a blanket over him, which was more merciful than to swim him through freezing water.

Dec^r. *19*th. Walked to DuG——'s, where we were told that the Wabash was impassible because the Ice was floating down in such great quantities.

Sent Isaac back with the packhorse and walked on to the river. The masses of ice filled the current of the stream, and broke against the shore, like harsh and distant Thunder.

*20*th. *21*st. *Dec*^r. At the cottage of the ferryman. This cabin contains but one room 12 feet square. The owner is a Canadian Frenchman, and he and

---

[1] John Smeaton (1724-1792) was an English civil engineer who made notable experiments on the power of water and air to turn mills and other machinery requiring a circular motion. His chief fame came from his rebuilding of the Eddystone lighthouse after its destruction by fire in 1755. This is the achievement to which Fordham refers.

his wife are very civil to us. We have two blankets and a buffalo robe on which we sleep with our feet to the fire.

Three men on the opposite shore, have, at the risk of their lives, crossed over amidst the ice. They were nearly two hours making unsuccessful efforts. They relanded, and lighted a fire. In the afternoon they tried again and dashed across. Their Canoe was nearly bored through, and half filled with Ice, which broke over them. They described the grinding of the Ice terrible.

I believe I should try, but my guns are valuable; and though B——d and myself might save ourselves, we should inevitably lose them if the Canoe should upset.

There is more genuine kindness and politeness among these backwoodsmen, than among any set of people, I have yet seen in America. They know so well the value of good neighbourhood, and feel so independent of the laws and restraints of every kind. Each man has a consciousness of power to do good or evil. Thus he is polite, for the same reason that the most powerful animals are gentle.

Canadian French Words

Freit, s.	cold	aussite		likewise
Mui,	me	icite	for	ici
orea, s.	ear	L'isle. s.	for	l'oeil
bain. ad.	good			

The river upon which Detroit is built is thickly settled for 60 leagues.[1]

---

[1] Detroit is located on a broad stream of the same name connecting Lakes Huron and Erie. Its site was regarded as strategic by the earliest French explorers, as La Salle, but a permanent post

The Hurons and Iroquois are Catholics.

Mocassins are sewed with the sinews of the Deer.

There are a few Indian slaves in Detroit.

23ᵈ. Crossed the Wabash in the afternoon in a Canoe amidst the Ice. Walked to the Swamp; but it was too dark for us to find the way across, and the Ice was rapidly thawing. After making three attempts we held a Council, whether it would be best to camp out upon a neck of land running into the Swamp, or to go back some miles to the only hut on that side the Swamp. We decided on the latter, as the melting snow would have made it impossible to light a fire, and it was then raining hard. The whistling of the wind and the howling of the wolves, all seemed to promise a stormy night. After cutting up my gun case to cover my thin Mocassins, which did not sufficiently protect my feet, we slowly retraced our steps, and reached Mʳ. A——'s cabin at 10. Found all the inhabitants abed, but not asleep. The room was so full of children, hunters, hogdrivers, and dogs, that it was with difficulty we could stretch our bodies upon the floor. There on our wet great coats, with our own wet blankets laid over us, we slept as soundly as ever I have slept on a featherbed.

was not established there until 1701, when Fort Pontchartrain was constructed by De la Mothe Cadillac. A settlement of French and Indians was begun, and by 1750 the place had a population of five hundred, with fully two thousand Indians living in the immediate neighborhood. Between 1760, when it passed under English control, and 1813, when it was finally reclaimed from British possession after Hull's surrender, the town had a history whose interest and significance it would be difficult to exaggerate. The story is told in many places, among them being Farmer's *History of Detroit and Michigan* (Detroit, 1884).

Next morning, proceeded at day break in a pelting shower to the swamp, with a man who was going the same way. Found a Canoe half full of Ice, and brimfull of water. Bailed it dry with our hands, and with difficulty launched it. After working hard in breaking the ice, and having our bodies completely drenched in perspiration, though our feet were very cold, we left the canoe, trusting ourselves to the Ice, and reached M^r. C——'s house, where we breakfasted and hired two horses, to take us to Princeton at Christmas Eve.

It was not expected we should have crossed the Wabash.

Christmas Day—This day was spent by one set of the *religionists* in hearing a sermon and prayers which lasted from breakfast till nightfall.

Another set of people were busy in cooking wild turkeys, and dancing in the evening.

The young men had their rifles out, and were firing feux de joi almost all the preceding night, all the day till late into the evening. It reminded me of Byron's description of the Moslems firing at the feast of the Ramadan in Constantinople:[1]—but we backwoodsmen never fire a gun loaded with *ball into* the town,—only from all parts of it, out towards the woods.

26th.—The Ball—There were about 20 couples: most of them genteelly dressed. We had Judge —— there with his daughter, with whom I

---

[1] The reference is obscure. The poem entitled *The Giaour* contains a passage which may have been in the writer's mind.

danced. There were no thin shoes to be obtained in the town, so we young men agreed to dance in Mocassins; some of which, made by the Indians, gaily embroidered and hung with little tassels of hair dyed red looked very smart.

27th & 28th. — Planning the Mill.

January 18th. 1818. I have been making a model of a Windmill, which is now nearly completed. The weather has been cold, but the air clear and chearful. The Thermometer once down to 8 below zero; but afterwards the air gradually became milder, till yesterday at noon it rose to 57°., and at night was 48°.

Several families have passed through the town for the Illinois, and every thing is going on so favorably, that all are chearful.

A repeal of the old law against duelling has been obtained, and a new one enacted which subjects delinquents to corporal punishments, in addition to the other penalties of fine and disability to hold public offices.. Col. E. drew up this bill.

This bill was thrown out at the third reading. The subject is involved in more difficulty, than it is in Europe. Every State has attempted to put a stop to duelling, and some have nearly effected it; but the manners and dispositions have not become more moderate or more mild. There are a number of dissipated and desperate characters, from all parts of the world, assembled in these Western States; and these, of course, are overbearing and insolent. It is nearly impossible for a man to be so circumspect, as to avoid giving offence to these irritable spirits; who, in fact, do not always wait for provocation to be insolent. The Kentuckians on these occasions use their dirks, and the Ohio men are abusive. Men of education and manners, will, if they can, fight with weapons; and the vulgar bite, kick, and gouge each other.

A new County has been made South of us; and Evansville, it is expected, will be the County Seat.[1]

There are Pelicans on the Wabash.

Rode this afternoon with Mess**. H——— and S——— through the Seminary Township,[2] which will

---

[1] This was Vanderburgh County, separated from Warrick by the state legislature early in 1818. In 1812 Hugh McGary, of Kentucky, built a log-house on the site of the future Evansville, which was the first dwelling erected by a white man in this section of the Indiana Territory. In 1816 General Robert M. Evans and James W. Jones purchased the land lying north of the present Main Street and laid out a town. Three years later the place had a hundred inhabitants, but thereafter it grew slowly (as late as 1830 having a population of only five hundred) until about the time of its incorporation in 1847, when it began a steady development which has made it second in size only to Indianapolis among the cities of the state. General Evans, the founder, was a Virginian who in 1803 settled at Paris, Kentucky, and two years later removed to a farm two miles north of the present town of Princeton, Indiana. From 1809 to 1811 he kept a hotel at Vincennes, but with the exception of these two years and 1824-25, which were spent at Evansville, he remained the rest of his life at his Gibson County location.

[2] In 1804 Congress bestowed upon the Territory of Indiana a township of land to be used for the establishment of a seminary of learning. Two years later Albert Gallatin, then Secretary of the Treasury, selected for this purpose a township, comprising 23,040 acres, in what is now Gibson County, and in 1807 the Territorial Legislature passed an act incorporating an institution "to be called or known by the name or style of the Vincennes University," and to be supported by lotteries and by the sale of land in the "seminary township." About 4,000 acres of the land were sold, a brick building was erected, and in 1810 the "university" was opened. Funds soon ran low, however, and in 1823 the school was forced to close its doors. In the following year it was declared extinct by the

be probably sold in a year or two. The land we crossed was excellent. Sugar tree, Elm, Oak, Hickory, and Sassafras mixed together. The Surface —rolling—and several fine eminences for houses. H—— has proposed to me to go to the South with him to join Gen. Gaines,[1] who is fighting with the

legislature. Meanwhile, in 1816, in the enabling act of Congress authorizing the formation of a state government for Indiana, the commonwealth was given another township, to be designated by the President of the United States, for the maintenance of a seminary. The township selected by President Monroe lay in what is now Monroe County and was later named Perry Township. In January, 1820, the Indiana legislature passed an act to establish a State Seminary. The site selected by the trustees of the prospective institution was the town of Bloomington, situated on the northern edge of the new "seminary township." In 1824 the Seminary was opened under the direction of Rev. Baynard R. Hall, who for three years was the only instructor. In January, 1828, the legislature raised the institution to the rank of a college and the presidency was vested in Dr. Andrew Wylie, then President of Washington College, Pennsylvania. By act of February 25, 1838, Indiana College was converted into Indiana University. In 1822 the legislature passed an act authorizing the sale of the remainder of the seminary township in Gibson County and providing for the application of the proceeds to the support of the Seminary created two years before. This act was defended on the ground that the trustees of the Vincennes University had sold a portion of their land in an illegal manner and had suffered their organization to lapse. It was keenly resented, however, by the friends of the defunct college and after the resurrection of the school in 1840 its new trustees brought suit against the purchasers of the Gibson County land to recover possession. In 1846 the legislature, recognizing the injustice of allowing the burden of defense of titles to rest on the purchasers, authorized the university to bring suit against the state. The outcome was a decision by the Supreme Court of the United States six years later in favor of the university; whereupon the state made due compensation for the lands thus virtually adjudged to have been confiscated. Vincennes University still exists as a minor college, though its persistent demands to be recognized as an institution having a just claim upon the state for support have been uniformly ineffective.

[1] In 1816-17 General Edmund P. Gaines was occupied on the Florida frontier with the difficult task of preserving order and checking the depredations of runaway negro slaves, Spanish and English filibusters, and various groups of hostile Indians. There ensued a period of border warfare, which culminated in the Seminole War of 1818, marked by the dashing operations of General Andrew Jackson.

Creek Indians. I declined the honour, and I believe he has relinquished his design.

Jany. 19th. Thermometer 54°. The morning opened with a thunderstorm. The day has been darker than any we have had this winter. I have yet seen no mists, except on the great rivers.

Jany. 23^d. Commenced my journey to Cincinnati. Slept at Vincennes.

—— *24th*. — *Sunday*. — Slept at M^{rs}. H's. Killed an Opossum on the road. Weather cold and rainy.

—— *25th*. — *Monday* — Slept at Bar's between the forks of White River.[1] Road dreadfully bad. The Prairie, or rather barren, for it is covered with shrubs, is pretty good land lying on clay, which gets so soft in wet weather, that the Horse's foot sinks deep into it. Once my horse sunk in the plain up to his chest, and rolled over.

Snow in evening.

26th. Crossed the East fork of White River and slept at D^r. A——'s. . . .

I made myself very comfortable here, and slept, for the first time in many months, between a pair of sheets. These are, however, no luxuries, compared with a clean and rather fine blanket.

A few miles from D^r. A——'s a river gushes from the ridge of rocky hills to the North, at once in its full size. Seventeen miles further North, a stream apparently as large, sinks into the hills. These are

---

[1] The East Fork of White River rises in Rush County, in southeastern Indiana, and the West Fork in Madison County, in the central part of the same state. The two unite near the town of Petersburg, about eighteen miles south-east of Vincennes.

1 0

probably one and the same. Last summer I rode with —— over that ridge, and missed both rivers. We passed some wildernesses, which seemed to be the abode of nothing but wild beasts; yet there while I was thinking of camping out, being quite lost, I found a habitation and a welcome.

It is reported that 250 warriors are assembled on the head waters of the White River, to avenge the deaths of some men, who have been murdered near this place.

Judge —— of —— overtaking me, informed me that the road to Cincinnati through Indiana was too bad to be travelled with safety.

I then changed my route, and set off with him. We swam Cane Creek and another little rapid stream. My mare swam by jerks, and dipped me waist deep. It was freezing hard, so that our clothes soon became stiff, and our horses were bearded with icicles.

Our road then lay over some high, rocky hills, which afforded distant prospects. We passed the mouths of some caverns, out of which rushed some mountain torrents.

America, however, is not the land of prospects. There is too much wood; and, when on the barren peak of some rocky hill, you catch a distant view, it generally is nothing but an undulating surface of impenetrable forests. The very views which are admired by the few Americans who have taste proves to me that North America is not generally picturesque.

Perhaps some parts of the mountains of Virginia and Kentucky would present exceptions; and the great rivers during the summer season. The footsteps of man, in spite of all the nonsense that has been written and said to the contrary, leave behind them beauty and delight. When the forests recede from the valleys, and verdure clothes the hills, and villages are scattered through wastes, North America will become a beautiful and picturesque country.

It is seldom that a view of 200 yards in extent, can be caught in Indiana. The woods west of the Mountains are not, as M^{rs}. W. says in the *wrongs* of woman, "clustering forests of small trees." It is a long time before an English eye becomes accustomed to their size and grandeur. The live poplar, or tulip-bearing tree, of which canoes are made, the sycamore, the walnut, and the white oak, grow to a prodigious size.

Four miles from Cane Creek we struck into a new path, which led over the tops of one of these knobs, which was composed chiefly of sandstone, with some argillaceous schist. The trees were covered with ice, so transparent and so brilliant, that the boughs looked like glasswork, and threw on the eye a confused splendour, which was bounded only by the distant hills. The boughs and fretwork of ice, that intercepted the rays of the sun, were faintly tinged with prismatic colours. At our feet were rapid torrents, which gushed from the cav-

erns above us, sparkled in light, and then leaped
into the darkness of the abysses below.

Another hour brought us to French-lick creek,[1]
where we dressed and warmed ourselves, and hired
a guide to take us to a fordable crossing. We carried our blankets and saddle bags in our arms, and
walked over a fallen tree, which tottered high in
air above the flood, and our guide drove our horses
after us through the river. This young man was
a cripple, and the second I have seen in the Western Country. Deformity is as rare among the
Backwoodsmen, as it is among the Indians.

We slept at M'. H——'s on —— Creek, a substantial Indiana farmer. He came home while we
were at supper, with three of his neighbours, who
were completely armed. They had been to take
some men to Paoli gaol, for robbing a store on
Little Blue river.[3] They informed us that there
were a gang of brigands on that river, who lived
by passing forged notes, stealing horses &c., and
hunting. They had a strong rock house among

[1] The sulphurous saline springs at French Lick became at an
early date one of the best known features of southern Indiana.
They are located in Orange County, about forty-five miles northwest of New Albany. Hulme, who visited them in 1818, says in his
Journal: "On our way [from Princeton to New Albany], pass
French Lick, a strong spring of water impregnated with salt and
sulphur, and called Lick from its being resorted to by cattle for the
salt; close by this spring is another still larger, of fine clear limestone water, running fast enough to turn a mill" (EARLY WESTERN
TRAVELS, x, p. 62). The stream thus originated is the creek to
which Fordham refers. The French Lick and neighboring West
Baden springs are now health resorts of considerable note.

[2] Paoli, the seat of Orange County, Indiana, is forty miles northwest of New Albany.

[3] Little Blue River is a small stream in southern Indiana, flowing
into the Ohio at a point about seventy-five miles below Louisville.

the hills, and it was said they had three or four
guns apiece. One of M^r. H——'s guests wanted to
raise the whole force of the settlement that night,
and to make an attack on the rock house before
daylight. But more prudent councils prevailed.
My companion Judge —— is a lively, entertaining young man; 24 years old. He is an *associate*
Judge and sits on the bench with the circuit or law
judge; but gives his opinion only on the equity of
a case. He is a merchant and a store keeper. He
rides a good horse with silver studded bridle, and
his saddle is ornamented with silver, and scarlet
housings. He carried a pair of pistols at his saddle
bow; and altogether looks more like a Dragoon
Officer in plain clothes, than a Judge. At least,
he is not at all like Lords Mansfield or Ellenbor-
ough.

27th. Breakfasted at M^r. C.——'s — another substantial farmer. He was at Corydon;[1] being a rep-
resentative of his fellow citizens in the Legislature.
His wife and sister soon cooked us an excellent
breakfast of Venison, Fowls, ham and bacon, hot
johnney cakes, waffles &c. We had likewise tea
and coffee, and a dram of whiskey, to keep the cold
off our stomachs. Our horses had 2 gallons of
oats. For all of which we paid 37½ Cents.

The country is still hilly, though not so broken
as that we crossed yesterday.

---

[1] Corydon, seat of Harrison County, became the capital of Indiana
in 1813. Twelve years later, and nine after the Territory had become a state, the capital was transferred to Indianapolis. See p. 101,
note.

Soil — third rate, — except in the bottoms. We crossed the Little Blue River at Fredericksburg, a miserable village, in a mud hole. The river is 50 yards wide, deep, and has a rapid current. It is called blue from the tint of the waters, which are clear and flow over a slaty bottom.

The land around Fredericksburg is high, and some of it sandy. It is inconceivable that the Americans should be so stupid as to plant their towns in the dirtiest puddles they can find. But they have such a dread of a little trouble, that they must be near a creek, that they may dip for water at their Cabin doors; for wells won't dig themselves, and the swing pole and bucket are for ever out of order. Pumps are out of all question with a backwoods man.

Ascending the hill from the forks of the Little Blue, we entered a high rolling country of sandy barrens. When we had passed these, we got entangled in a flat swampy tract of White oak land, which we were two hours crossing. At Sunset passed another little village of hewn log Cabins, and arrived at M^r. D——'s just as it got dark. . . .

Here we overtook a Captn. B—— from the upper parts of Kentucky, who joined Company with us.

28th. — About 8 miles from D——'s we ascended a high ridge, which gave us a view of the Ohio with its Silver waves gleaming in the Sun. Louisville[1] on the opposite banks 6 miles N. E. and the

---

[1] The first plot for a settlement on the site of Louisville was prepared in 1773 by Captain Thomas Bullitt, an agent sent out by the

hills of Kentucky, formed a waving outline of dark forests, and around and beneath us were steep banks thinly covered with timber.

Two hours brought us to Albany,[1] on the Ohio.

College of William and Mary to approve western surveys. Two years later the place was occupied, though the beginnings of the present city are really to be traced only to the pioneers who went to "the Falls" with George Rogers Clark in 1778 and eventually settled there (see note 1 below). By 1784 the town comprised a hundred houses and thanks to the growing traffic up and down the Ohio and to the rapids which compelled a portage near its site, was well on the road to prosperity (on the Falls, see p. 105, note 2). Cuming, in his *Sketches*, written in 1808, describes the place as follows: "Louisville consists of one principal and very handsome street, about half a mile long, tolerably compactly built, and the houses generally superior to any I have seen in the western country with the exception of Lexington. Most are of handsome brick, and some are three stories, with a parapet wall on the top in the modern European taste, which in front gives them the appearance of having flat roofs. I had thought Cincinnati one of the most beautiful towns I had seen in America, but Louisville, which is almost as large, equals it in beauty, and in the opinion of many excells it" (Early Western Travels, iv, pp. 259-260). Melish tells us, in 1811, that the town had a population of 1307, including 484 negro slaves (*Travels*, ii, pp. 149-150). By 1820 the population had increased to over 4000, and by 1826 to over 7000. Travellers were generally very favorably impressed with the location of the town and with the character of its people. Among interesting accounts may be mentioned Fearon, *Sketches*, pp. 245-255; Woods, *Two Years' Residence* (Early Western Travels, x, pp. 242-244); William Tell Harris, *Remarks*, pp. 129-130, 143-145; Faux, *Memorable Days* (Early Western Travels, xi, p. 196); Welby, *Visit to North America* (Early Western Travels, xii, pp. 226-227); and Ogden, *Letters from the West* (Early Western Travels, xix, pp. 40-41). On the history of Louisville see Reuben Thomas Durrett, *The Centenary of Louisville*, Filson Club Publications No. 8 (Louisville, 1893); H. McMurtrie, *Sketches of Louisville and its Environs* (Louisville, 1819); and Ben Casseday, *History of Louisville from its Earliest Settlement till the Year 1852* (Louisville, 1852).

[1] Albany, now known as New Albany, is the seat of Floyd County, Indiana. The history of the town begins in a sense with the grant of 150,000 acres of land in its vicinity to the officers and soldiers of George Rogers Clark's Illinois regiment, made by the legislature of Virginia in 1783. Clarksville, across the Ohio from Shippingport and a little above the mouth of Silver Creek, was established in pursuance of this grant. The site selected was not a healthful one, however, and for various reasons the settlement did not prosper; in 1819 it contained fewer than one hundred people. The place is now a suburb of New Albany. The latter town proper was

Its Main Street is a broad ditch of mud. We crossed the Ohio here, and took leave of Judge ——. Captn. B—— and myself went on to Louisville.

We put up at the Washington Hall, a handsome hotel; supplied apparently with the usual luxuries of European Inns, except clean floors. There were a great many well-dressed gentlemen in the reading and bar room, whose attention was caught by my appearance. I had on a decent suit of clothes, though past their best, and a pair of Kentucky leggings, but over my great coat I wore a blanket, pinned under the chin in the Indian fashion, and confined to the waist by a leather belt; to which was suspended a large hunting or scalping Knife. Fifteen years ago, this was a common dress in Kentucky, as it is now on the frontiers of Indiana and in the Illinois Territory. But the early Settlers of Kentucky are dead, or moved farther west; or have become rich and luxurious, and Mercantile adventurers have introduced the fashions of London and Paris. Perhaps there is a greater proportion of well dressed men in Louisville than in any European Commercial city.

We remounted our horses again at 4 p. m., and at dark we reached the habitation of Monsr. N., who keeps a house of private entertainment, that is to say, an Inn; in which travellers are received, but neighbours are not allowed to drink.

laid out by Messrs. Scribner, its proprietors, in 1814. Being located on the second bank of the river, it was found satisfactory from the standpoint of healthfulness, and within half a dozen years it had come to have a population of one thousand. Thereafter its growth was slow but steady.

These houses are more comfortable than Inns, and are generally a little cheaper. You take your Meals with the family, — retire into the strangers' room, as soon as the meal is over, — and generally the master of the house follows to chat with you. You are not expected to call for liquors; which, indeed, are not often kept in the house. . . .[1]

To avoid sleeping with a bedfellow in a small bed, I wrapped myself up in my blanket and laid on my great coat and Saddle bags before the fire. This arrangement disconcerted two Negro slaves, who had chosen that place for themselves. I obliged them to sleep at some distance.

Negroes are never supplied with more bedding than a blanket and the Kitchen or dining room floor. This too in Kentucky; which is the Paradise of slaves, compared with the Southern States.

Jany. 30th. — We passed through a fertile country, well settled, but with miserably bad roads by Middleton,[2] to the flourishing little town of Shelbyville, in Shelby County.[3]

Here we met, at a good Inn, a large party of rich farmers and Merchants, all busy talking politics.

---

[1] "A page of the Journal here has been lost. The next day the Author and his companion proceeded on their journey and arrived at night at another house of entertainment." — TRANSCRIBER.

[2] Middleton is situated on the headwaters of Bear Grass Creek, twelve miles east of Louisville and twenty west of Shelbyville.

[3] Shelbyville and Shelby County take their names from Isaac Shelby, first governor of the state of Kentucky and one of the most notable personages in early Western history. Shelbyville is thirty miles east of Louisville and twenty west of Frankfort. Melish, in 1811, gives it a population of 424 (*Travels*, ii, p. 179). Faux, in 1818, describes it as a "good-looking, youthful town" (EARLY WESTERN TRAVELS, xi, p. 195).

The Landlord, finding I was an Englishman, invited me to spend the evening with his wife and daughters. I found them handsome and agreeable women. Our charge for Supper, breakfast, and horsefeed was $1,75cents. Hostler & boots got, 25c. Dearer travelling than in Indiana, where a dollar per day will pay all the expences. They may be stated thus:

	In Indiana Cents	*In Kentucky* Cents
Breakfast . . .	12½ .	. 25
Horsefeed . . .	12½ .	. 12½
D°. at noon .	. 12½ .	. 12½
Supper & horsefeed .	62½ .	. 1,00
	$1,00	$1,50

The above are the charges at houses of private entertainment. At good taverns the charges are at least 50 pr. Cent higher. If the badness of the roads, in the Winter, is taken into consideration, travelling at this Season is dearer than in England; for you cannot get half the distance in the same time.

In Summer the roads are, in general, good for travelling on horseback.

Jany. 31st. Started for Frankfort.[1] Passed

[1] The site of Frankfort was first surveyed in 1773 for the McAfee brothers. In October, 1786, it was purchased by James Wilkinson (see p. 62, note), who had secured the passage of a bill in the Virginia Assembly to erect a town upon it. The place was selected in 1793 to be the capital of the new state. Cuming visited it in 1807 and found a town of ninety houses, including a state-house, a jail, a court-house, a state penitentiary, a market-house, a gov-

through a fine rolling country; cleared enough to present something like views; though none of them of any extent.

Frankfort is a smart little town, on the Kentucky river. It is the seat of Government; and the Legislature is now sitting.

It was Sunday, and a few smartly dressed young men were picking their way through the half frozen mud in the streets. Like others it is hid in a mud hole, with fine commanding situations around it. They have begun to pave the Main Street — in a way that would make a London Paviour laugh.

The Kentucky River pours a noble stream over a bed of Limestone. It is crossed by a wooden bridge supported by four stone piers.[1] There is a good view from the Eastern bank, which rises abruptly, perhaps 100 feet, above the bed of the river. Its circuitous course winds among steep bluffs, south of the Town. In the plain above are several smart houses, pleasantly situated. They look like the places of Summer retreat, in which the Citizens of London indulge themselves on Sundays.

---

ernment house, and four inns which in size, accommodations, and business he declares were not surpassed in the United States (EARLY WESTERN TRAVELS, iv, pp. 191-196). Travellers generally compared Frankfort with Lexington, favorably as a rule to the former except in the matter of commercial facilities. See Faux, *Memorable Days* (EARLY WESTERN TRAVELS, xi, p. 174) and Welby, *Visit to North America* (EARLY WESTERN TRAVELS, xii, pp. 222-225).

[1] Cuming, in 1807, says: "The erection of a permanent wooden bridge over the Kentucky has been lately commenced, which will be about one hundred and forty yards long from bank to bank, the surface of which is about fifty feet above low water mark. The present bridge of boats is about sixty-five yards between the abutments, and the river now at low water is eighty-seven yards wide" (EARLY WESTERN TRAVELS, iv, p. 193).

Five miles further, we put up at M[r]. B——s'
house. A respectable and venerable man, who has
been thirty four years in Kentucky. His lady was
complaining bitterly of the Mal-practices of their
State Legislature, of their taxes &c, though the
latter are nothing more than County rates.

Monday Feb[y]. 2[d]. Took leave of Capt[n]. B——
who was going to Lexington,[1] crossing Elk horn
creek,[2] and struck N.W. among the Eagle creek
hills.[3] I soon left the fertile plains of Kentucky.

[1] The traditional story of the origin of Lexington (as told, for
example, in Melish's *Travels,* ii, p. 187, and accepted in Winsor's
Westward Movement, p. 85) to the effect that the first log cabins at
the place were built in 1775 and given the name Lexington in
honor of the battle lately fought between the Americans and British,
can hardly be regarded as true. It appears that there was no permanent settlement on the site of the present city before 1779. In
1780 the new town was made the seat of Fayette County and two
years later, it was incorporated by the legislature of Virginia. François André Michaux has a good description of the place in 1802
(EARLY WESTERN TRAVELS, iii, pp. 199-206). Cuming, in 1807,
writes a very full account (EARLY WESTERN TRAVELS, iv, pp. 181-
189). He estimates the town's population at three thousand and
has nothing but praise for its schools (including Transylvania University), churches, stores, and manufacturing enterprises. Melish,
in 1811, gives some interesting information (*Travels,* ii, pp. 185-
190). Two visitors in the year 1818 record the most contrary
impressions: Faux declares that every public building in the city,
save that of the University, was filthy, neglected, and falling into
ruins, and that though the place still contained the cream of Kentucky society it was thought to be retrograding (EARLY WESTERN
TRAVELS, xi, p. 188); but William Tell Harris was charmed with
all that he saw, and wrote that Lexington was "a spot so much
more pleasant, as well as more central, that it appears difficult to
conceive what could have induced the transfer of the legislative priv-
ilege to Frankfort, unless it be a supposed advantage in its being
washed by the waters of the Kentucky" (*Remarks,* pp. 145-146).
George W. Ranck's *History of Lexington* (Lexington, 1872) is a
fairly good work of its kind.

[2] Elkhorn Creek, on a branch of which Lexington is situated, flows
into the Kentucky River in Franklin County, about eight miles
north of Frankfort.

[3] Eagle Creek Hills are in the region north of Shelbyville and
twenty to thirty miles west of Frankfort.

The roads have been so bad, that my horse has been for two days much fatigued. Today he gave out, and I with difficulty got him through the wilderness. I arrived at the house I am now writing in, and as the people seem to be civil and courteous, I shall rest tomorrow.

A Traveller, who has been four or five months in the wildernesses of the Illinois Territory, or the gloomy forests of Indiana, is delighted with the fine clearings of the Kentucky farms. Yet these seldom extend half a mile from the road, and that the most public one from Louisville to Lexington. Hence there are seldom any views that can be called picturesque in that tract of country which lies within 50 miles of Ohio. There are some that are grand and solemn among the hills, but in the rich country, the stumps of trees in the fields, the worm rail-fences running in straight lines, and even the forests, with their rigid outlines as left by the axe, have little of beauty and still less of the picturesque. It is the feeling that he is surrounded by the dwellings of man, that cheers the lonely traveller.

The Kentuckians[1] have the character of being the best warriors of the United States. As far as courage without conduct can make them soldiers, they are deserving of this praise.

---

[1] Other accounts of the life and society of Kentucky in the early part of the last century are F. A. Michaux, *Travels* (EARLY WESTERN TRAVELS, iii, p. 222, ff.) ; Cuming, *Sketches* (EARLY WESTERN TRAVELS, iv, p. 165, ff.) ; Melish, *Travels*, ii, pp. 202-208; Fearon, *Sketches*, pp. 237-255; Flint, *Letters* (EARLY WESTERN TRAVELS, ix, p. 132, ff.) ; Faux, *Memorable Days* (EARLY WESTERN TRAVELS, xi, p. 188, ff.) ; and Ogden, *Letters from the West* (EARLY WESTERN TRAVELS, xix, pp. 94-102). Cf., pp. 177-181 and 214-216 of this volume.

They pride themselves on their veracity and honour.

In their persons they are large, and generally handsome, but are too much inclined to corpulency. *Tuesday and Wednesday.* My horse being unable to proceed, I staid two days at M^r. T——'s, a Kentucky farmer of the middle class. He works himself and employs two Negroes. Every thing around him bespoke comfort and moderate wealth. Yet he has cultivated his own land among these hills only 10 years. His farm is productive, though far from being so rich as the level plains.

He talks of moving out to the Illinois Territory. *Feby. 5th. Thursday.* Rode to M^r. H——'s Tavern, with whom I spent a most agreeable evening. He rents a farm for which he pays one third of the produce. He talked of mechanics, and is going to erect a carding machine.

Feby. 6th. Friday. Rode to M^r. G——'s. At this house I met M^r. S——, a member of the Senate, and other interesting gentlemen.

The bridge of Frankfort cost 40,000$. One is projected over the mouth of Licking at Newport,[1] which will cost as much. Another is talked of to be thrown over the Ohio, at the expense of 300,000$.

---

[1] The Licking River rises in south-eastern Kentucky, near the sources of the Cumberland and Kentucky. It flows through a course of some two hundred miles, but is of slight value for navigation during all but two months of the year. Newport, the seat of Campbell County, was platted in 1791 by General James Taylor, a recent emigrant from Caroline County, Virginia. It was incorporated and made seat of justice in 1795, and in 1803 the Government selected it as a location for an arsenal. Covington, on the west bank of the Licking, opposite Newport, was founded in 1815.

Feby. 7th.   Crossed the Ohio and arrived at Cincinnati.[1] Called on my friend ———. Told him my wish to obtain private lodgings; which he got for me in a most respectable quaker family. He offered me too, his interest in the Library of Cincinnati. . . .

Feby. 23^d. The City Guards, who are a uniform company of volunteers, are parading the town in celebration of the birthday of Washington, which fell yesterday on Sunday.

A grand ball will be given tonight, to which I shall not go, as I do not choose the risk of being insulted by any vulgar Ohioans. . . .

I send you a map of the Illinois territory. It is tolerably correct, being taken from the Office Map.

Feby. 26th. We have had a launch of a Steam boat today of 150 Tons burthen. It was a beautiful sight; she plunged bows under, as the bilge way was at the lowest end eight feet above the water.

---

[1] On Cincinnati, see p. 183, note.

IX

A trip across the Wabash in search of land — A night in the woods — The people of Indiana — The Kentuckians.

At a farm house among the Eagle Creek Hills;
30 miles West from Frankfort, Kentucky.

Feby. 3. 1818.

As general descriptions of Countries give always vague and unsatisfactory ideas, I will fill up this sheet with extracts from [my] Journal, which I hope will be amusing. You will keep in mind, the *truth* of a picture depends much upon the slightest touches, and that resemblance cannot be produced but by attention to minutiee.

Soon after my return from Cincinnati in September, I went across the Wabash to seek some good timbered land. I went alone on horseback, carrying my American Rifle, which is a long gun, weighing 10 lbs, and shoots a bullet of ¼ oz weight. I had a clean shirt and stockings in my saddle bags, and provisions for four days; a bag of Indian corn for my horse, a blanket, a cloak, and tin cup; a pocket compass, a map of the country, a large hunting Knife, and a hatchet.

The first day's ride brought me to a swampy, flat prairie, which I crossed just as the sun went down. I turned into a thick wood, where the trees were small and close together. I was then a poor woodsman, or I should have chosen a better place. I lighted a fire with brush wood, and then began cutting down some small trees.

I had nearly finished the second, when my hatchet flew off the handle. During the time I spent in looking in vain for it, the fire went out and it got quite dark.

I was in a bad *fix*, as they say in the back woods. However, I made the best of it; fed my horse, eat my supper, and wrapped myself up warm, hugging my gun in my blanket. I lay listening a good while, and had fallen into a doze, when my horse snorted, and my dog jumped up, and I heard something rush through the woods at, perhaps, 100 yards distance. All was still again, — but the winds whistling through the trees, and now and then a wolf howling afar off. I lay down again, and soon fell asleep.

The next morning I struck a path which led to a Cabin where I breakfasted on hominy and honey, and proceeded across the Boon-pas, up the long Prairie 2 miles. I then took the woods, and, after struggling five hours among grape vines and creeks, I found some Whiteoak timbered land near our prairie. I ran the section line, then crossed the prairie to the North end, and reached M^r. E.——— at dark.

The next day I found still better land, well timbered. Found the section line and started off for Shawnee town, which I reached in two days.

Here I entered land; and soon after went again to the Prairie to get a cabin built, and returned to Shawnee. . . .

I hope you will not think this letter is filled with

11

matter unworthy of being sent across the Atlantic. These minute descriptions alone can give you an idea of these wildernesses.

The farmers of Indiana generally arrive in the country very poor, but somehow they get a great deal of property very soon. They all work, and there are not half so many labourers for hire, as there are farmers. The former live with their employers, and are their equals, if they are men of good character; which is not always the case. The hunters have more politeness, and I think more of virtue and hospitality than the farmers. The worse set are boatmen, and petty traders in horses and whisky, who live on the banks of rivers. Some of these are connected with horse stealers and forgers, and are the pests of a rising society. The new towns on the frontiers generally are inhabited by these men, till they rise into importance; when the scamps move off. Though we have rascals even here, yet the tone of morals is higher on the frontiers, than among men of the same station in England. They are either very good or openly bad in these back woods.

I do not think much can be said in praise of the daughters of Indiana; they are completely destitute of education. Not so, the Kentucky women. From the little I have seen and the much I have heard, I judge they are the most spirited women in the world. They are exceedingly fond of dress, and are generally very handsome. But Kentucky is growing very rich, and the people are becoming very proud.

I shall reserve my observations on Kentucky for a future letter, and likewise a geographical and statistical sketch of the South Eastern section of the Illinois Territory.[1]

Either Kentucky or Illinois must be the abode of an English farmer. In the one he will find an agreeable society, in the other there is none, and he will give to it, as it rises, a tint of his own manners.

Cincinnati. Feby. 14th. . . . . Land has been sold near this town for 200$ per acre.—45£. The people cannot be poor who buy or sell such land. Yet twenty-two years ago, this land was the property of the Indians, and the few white men who lived here, dared not leave their fort. Still if it were not for Slavery, Kentucky or Virginia would be the countries for English Gentlemen. A Kentuckian is an Englishman with a little more pride.

---

[1] For the promised observations on Kentucky see pp. 177-181, and pp. 214-216. There does not appear in the manuscript any systematic sketch of the Illinois Territory, but much valuable information and comment is given incidentally here and there.

X

The Americanizing of emigrants — Attitude of Westerners toward Englishmen — Prospective peace with the southern Indians — Emigration to Missouri — Mr. Birkbeck's estate — Fordham's farm — Opportunities for men with capital — Respect for education and manners.

Cincinnati Feby. 18. 1818.

I TAKE a hasty opportunity of sending you a few lines by a gentleman who is going to Scotland from this place. He will start tomorrow morning early; and I have to give a dozen orders to Engineer, Smiths and founders in the course of the day; so you will excuse a very hastily written scrawl.

We are all in good health and spirits, and are more accustomed to American manners; — therefore more comfortable. It is useless for Emigrants to think of retaining English manners or English feelings, in this country of liberty and *equality*. But, to do the Americans justice, they respect the love, which every man of generous feeling has for his native country, and they are pretty in expressing their contempt of a Renegado. There are too many of this character; and I have been more hurt by their conduct, than by all the rudeness of the Ohioans, or the pride and haughtiness of Kentuckians.

The Western Americans generally feel great hostility to the British Government, but towards the English Emigrants, they are, with few exceptions, kind and hospitable. They are in most respects different from their brethren in the East, for whom they do not entertain much respect or affection.

Military courage is here considered to be the prince of all the virtues. Even quakers talk like soldiers, and frequently the younger members turn out with their fellow citizens.

The Indians in the South, who were making a great head against Gen. Gaines, have now proposed a friendly talk, and, probably, peace will be concluded before this reaches you. I am glad of this, because there was some danger of the spirit of hostility spreading among the tribes who live on the Western banks of the Mississippi, and the Northern tribes. In that case we must have fortified our dwellings; and we young men, though not called upon by law, should have looked small if we had not volunteered.

The prophet chief, brother of Tecumseh,[1] is still living beyond the Missouri. The Missouri Territory is peopling so fast, that very soon our country

---

[1] The Prophet was a Shawnee warrior, known in early life as Lawlewasikaw, but after assuming the prophetic role in 1805 as Pemsquatawah. With this change of name and profession he began to make himself conspicuous by declaiming against witchcraft, the use of intoxicating liquors, intermarriage with the whites, and the selling of Indian lands to the United States. Late in 1805, or early in 1806, he and his brother Tecumseh removed from the Delaware villages on the west fork of White River (in present Delaware County, Indiana) to Greenville, Ohio; and in the spring of 1808 they gained permission of the Pottawattamies and Kickapoos to settle on the Wabash near the mouth of the Tippecanoe, at a place which afterwards bore the name of the Prophet's Town. While the Prophet's fame and influence grew among the tribes of northwestern Indiana, Tecumseh busied himself with efforts to unite these tribes in one great confederacy on the basis of a common resistance to the encroachments of the whites. Relations between the Indian leaders and the representatives of the national government, chiefly Governor William Henry Harrison, became more and more strained, until in

will be backed up on that side. The banks of the Okaw[1] and the Little Muddy,[2] about 80 miles westward of us, are entering very fast, though unluckily by Speculators, as well as settlers. We have as yet, however, been fortunate enough to keep the former away from our immediate neighbourhood.

An English gentleman of fortune, a M[r]. Q——, is gone down the river with his family, with the intention of buying land close to us.

M[r]. Birkbeck is laying out a farm of 1600 acres in the midst of his Estate of 4000 acres. He has entered the whole of the Bolton house prairie; with the exception of three quarters on the South West side, and one quarter on the North side of M[r]. Flower's land, which I have entered for myself.

My little Estate lies on and between two small hills, from which descend several small streams, that unite in the valley and flow on through the prairie. An arm of the prairie runs up this valley and extends itself on the heights somewhat in this shape.[3] I suppose I have about 100 acres of meadow and 60 of timber land. The timber is white oak,

---

1811 the crisis came in the noted battle of Tippecanoe in which the Indians were defeated and the confederacy shattered. Tecumseh joined the British the following year and was killed in the battle of the Thames, October 5, 1813. The Prophet removed to the Indian country on the western side of the Mississippi, where he died in 1834. A good account of the careers of these rather remarkable redskins will be found in John B. Dillon's *History of Indiana* (Indianapolis, 1859), pp. 423-553 *passim*.

[1] The Okaw is a small tributary of the Kaskaskia, in Washington County, Illinois.

[2] The Little Muddy flows into the Big Muddy in the eastern part of Jackson County, Illinois. The Big Muddy enters the Mississippi in northwestern Union County.

[3] See sketch on opposite page.

walnut, and Hickory. There are some Persimmons, a most delicious fruit, growing on straight and rather lofty trees, a good many grapes and hazels.

I am getting the iron work for a wind-mill, and other machinery. Iron costs 12½ c^{ts}. per lb, and the working is charged at 12½ c^{ts}. more. I have bought anvils, bellows, and all the tools of a Blacksmith's, Millwright's, and Carpenter's shop. I can get work done here as well as in London at from 50 to 100 per Cent advance upon London prices.

I am going down the river in a boat of which I shall take the command. I went down last Autumn in two boats, in one of which I had two horses. To confess the truth I nearly lost the boats and all the property would have been gone, if my lads had not made uncommon exertions. It was in the night and a most tremendous thunder storm came on. The intervals between the flashes of lightning were so dark that we could not see some rocks, which we ran foul of, and hung to all night.

I am boarding in a very respectable quaker family, who do not in general take in boarders. But I was recommended by a gentleman of this town, with whom I had travelled, and to whom we are all well known. Introductions into respectable families are as necessary in this country as in any other; and as much is thought of steadiness of conduct, though more latitude is given to speech.

I have consciously avoided giving to my young friends in England coloured descriptions of this country: but I must beg leave to assure you — that you cannot do a greater favour to any young man, who possesses from 800£ to 5,000£, with a proper degree of spirit, than by sending him out here. But if he has no money, if he knows no mechanical trade, and if he cannot work, — he had better stay in a Counting house in England.

Any young man, who wishes to marry, but dare not enter into business and the expences of a family in England, if he can command 1000£, may choose his trade here. If he is a plain working farmer, 500£ will make him more independent than an English gentleman with 1000£ per annum.

An Emigrant who is rich, may settle near a large town; find society, libraries, and a great many comforts. If he does not object to holding Slaves, Kentucky offers him great advantages. But if he is not rich, or is ambitious, — the Illinois and Missouri Territory, and, from what I have heard, I may say, the Alabama Country, will hold out advantages that will pay him for all sacrifices.[1]

A bill is in Congress for making a State of the Illinois Territory.[2] We shall be Citizens as soon as it passes, and eligible I believe to any office.

[1] For more extended observations on the various regions which held out inducements to European emigrants see pp. 227-228.

[2] In January, 1818, the legislature of Illinois, through Nathaniel

Men of Education and Manners are much respected; and there is a large proportion of the people, who have a great deal of information; which though acquired more by conversation and observation, than by reading, makes them good judges of character, and enables them to value literary and scientific acquirements.

I have had interest offered me to procure an election to a command in a Militia regiment in Indiana; but I have declined the offer. . . .

Pope, the territorial delegate, petitioned Congress for admission to the Union. On the following eighteenth of April Congress passed the desired act enabling the people of the territory to frame a constitution and establish a state government. A noteworthy feature of this act was the provision that the northern boundary of the new state should be the line 40° 30′ N. Lat.— a provision secured by the efforts of Pope, who saw that if a line drawn through the southernmost point of Lake Michigan were made the boundary, as it had been assumed would be the case, the valuable port of Chicago would be lost to some state yet to be constituted on the north. The new line is about forty miles further north than the old one and the fourteen Illinois counties lying wholly or in part between the two were regarded by not a few Wisconsin people of a generation ago as wrongfully attached to the commonwealth on the south. August 26, 1818, a convention met at the capital, Kaskaskia, and framed a constitution, which was duly ratified. Shadrach Bond, a Marylander who had settled in Illinois at an early date, was elected first governor of the state. He assumed the duties of the office in October, 1818. In this same month the legislature had its first session and Ninian Edwards and Jesse B. Thomas were elected to the United States Senate. During an adjourned session, in the winter of 1818-19, a code of laws (borrowed in the main from the codes of Virginia and Kentucky) was adopted and commissioners were appointed to select a site for a new capital. The result of the latter act was the choice of Vandalia, occupied in 1821 (see p. 104, note 1).

XI

Cincinnati Feby. 26. 1818.

HAVING an opportunity of sending a letter by a private conveyance, I seize it with avidity, because I have great hope you will receive it safe. The post offices of this Western Country are so ill conducted that it is quite discouraging.

I need not tell you what we are doing, for M^r. Birkbeck's book[1] has told you already. We are proceeding steadily, though slowly. . . .

Now I will tell you a little of what I have seen and learnt; and that I may give you my ideas undisturbed, and fresh from my mind, I will not affect any sort of arrangement.

I have seen but little of Virginia. The men of education and wealth are much like English Country gentlemen, about as refined and nearly as proud. The young men are irascible but goodnatured. They are, however, rude and greedy in their manners at public tables to a most shameful degree.

The women are pretty, languishing, made-up misses. Their chief pleasures seem to be in dressing well and in combing their long fair hair. They

---

[1] Fordham here refers to Birkbeck's *Notes on a Journey in America from the Coast of Virginia to the Territory of Illinois* (Philadelphia, 1817).

have most beautiful hair, and are generally much fairer than English women. Like the men, they are tall and thin; but they have not the intelligent look of the former.

Kentucky, which is the daughter of Virginia, has fewer men of literary tastes and habits, but more men of enterprise, both commercial and military. Their military enthusiasm scarcely knows any limit. They are, without doubt, very brave, but the men of other States say they are not steady. It is certain that they have in the late war been at times most unaccountably panic-struck.

Kentucky, or "bloody field," was won inch by inch from the Indians;—by a few enterprising men, unaided by governments, unorganized, for the most part poor, and connected merely by mutual wants and interests. It was not the property of any particular tribe of Savages, but the disputed hunting ground of many. It was the theatre of their wars;—and was won from them by Boon and his associates contending with them in their own way.

Daniel Boon[1] first crossed the mountains on a hunting expedition in 1769, accompanied by 5 men. In 1772 his force did not amount to 100 men, and

---

[1] Daniel Boone was born in 1734 in the valley of the Schuylkill in Pennsylvania. In 1757 his family moved to Buffalo Lick, on the north fork of the Yadkin, in North Carolina. There he grew to manhood, becoming a hunter and backwoodsman of the most strenuous type. In 1769, with five companions, he pushed westward through Cumberland Gap and began the notable career in Kentucky which Fordham outlines. His later years were spent in the Missouri Territory, which became more attractive to him than Kentucky, owing to the rapidity with which the latter was increasing in

in the interval between these years he had been
living 18 months in the wilderness alone, clad in
bear skins, and often fearing to light a fire. He
had sent away his Companions for his family and
for powder.

You will never have a correct idea of what a
wilderness is till you come to visit me. It is no
more like a great wood, than a battle is like a review. Whatever limits it may have on the map,
however quickly the eye may traverse the chart,
or the imagination may skim over the fancied desert, — the traveller and hunter find impediments,
which give to him notions of extension.

To be at an unknown distance from the dwellings of man; to have pathless forests of trees
around you; and intervening rivers, across which
you must swim on your horse or on a raft, whatever be the temperature of the water or the air; —
the whispering breeze among the leaves, the spring
of the deer, or the flap of the Eagle's wing are the
only sounds you hear during the day; and then to
lie at night in a blanket, with your feet to a fire,
your rifle hugged in your arms, listening to the
howling wolves, and starting at the shriek of the
terrible panther: This it is to be in a Wilderness
alone.

To return to Daniel Boon, — and Kentucky — He
was twice taken prisoner by the Indians and

population. The removal to Missouri seems to have been made in
the spring of 1799. The best biography of Boone is Thwaites,
Daniel Boone (New York, 1902). William Harvey Miner's *Daniel
Boone: Contribution toward a Bibliography of Writings concerning Daniel Boone* (New York, 1901) is useful.

French, and once marched to Canada. He had been spared by the Indians because they admired his bravery. He escaped alone, and returned to his fort on Kentucky river. His wife and daughters, having been left by their husband, who had been surprised in the woods, had likewise left the fort desolate. Boon pushed on across the Mountains to N. Carolina, and found his family at a relation's house.

Battles with the Indians are a series of duels; it was so then, and is so now. A brave man kills the greatest number, and it is nothing to him, whether ten are engaged or a hundred. He only looks to do his own duty, and to get as many scalps as he can. The Kentuckians have adopted the Indian custom of scalping the dead.

Cassidy, an Irishman, — a smaller man, it is said, by people who know him, than I am, — is the next on the list of fame.[1] He has killed more men than Boon has, and most of them in single fights, or Indian hunting, as it is called. I believe he is alive yet. Boon has a settlement 280 miles west of us, has got a new rifle this season, — and is gone out to kill another bear before he dies: — he is 80 years old.

---

[1] Captain Michael Cassidy was a native of Ireland who migrated to the United States in his youth and won no small distinction as a soldier in the Revolution. At the close of the war he removed to Kentucky and settled at Cassidy's Station, in Fleming County. He was one of the most noted frontiersmen of his time. In connection with his diminutive stature, to which Fordham alludes, it may be said that numerous amusing stories are told regarding his encounters with Indians, who thought him to be a mere boy and treated him with corresponding condescension.

A wealthy Kentucky farmer has 20 or 30 slaves, whom he treats rather like children than servants, — 2 or 3000 acres of land, 500 acres of which are cleared and in cultivation. He lives in a bad house, keeps a plentiful table, which is covered three times a day with a great many dishes. Brandy, Whisky, and Rum are always standing at a side table. He is hospitable, but rather ostentatious, plain in his manners, and rather grave; a great politician, rather apt to censure than to praise, and a rather bigoted republican. It is said by enemies, that were a person to travel through Kentucky and openly approve of Monarchical principles, he would be stabbed. This is not true; but it is true that they are irascible, to a great degree, and it would not be wise for any man to preach up even federal, that is, tory, principles in this State.

Nothing is more common than for men in Kentucky to quarrel about politics, and the pistol used to be the universal resort. But as almost every duel was fatal, the legislature took effectual means to prevent duelling. The dirk is now generally worn, and not unfrequently used in the lower parts near the Tennessee line.

I, however, like Kentucky: — there is much to interest me in its inhabitants, though there is much to disapprove.

You have heard of the Mammoth Cave[1] — I have

---

[1] Mammoth Cave is in Edmonson County, Kentucky, about ninety-five miles southwest of Louisville. It was discovered accidentally by a hunter in 1809.

seen the skull of a Mammoth found in White River in Indiana — it is a tremendous head-piece. In the Illinois Country, Society is yet unborn, — but it will be soon. The western parts toward St. Louis are thickest settled, and with very dissipated characters. French and Indian traders, Canadians, &c, gamblers, horsestealers, and bankrupts. Near us there are only a few farmers and hunters. Farmers, who till their own land, shear their own sheep, grow their own cotton and tobacco, the former of which their wives manufacture into clothing through every process. They tan the hides of their cattle and deer skins, and make them up into shoes and harness. They are hospitable according to their means; but, if they live near roads, expect payment for food and lodging, which is rather demanded by travellers than accepted as a favour.

The hunters live rather worse, but are more entertaining and interesting companions. Clothed in *dressed* not *tanned* buckskins: — a home-made, homespun hunting shirt outside; — belted to his waist with a broad belt, to which is appended a knife with a blade a foot long: a tomohawk, or powder horn, in the belt of which is sometimes a smaller knife to cut the patch of the bullet; a bullet-pouch; mocassins on his feet; a blanket on his saddle; and a loaf of Indian Corn. Thus equipped and accoutered he enters the trackless woods, without a compass, or a guide, but what appears a kind of instinct. He is fearless of every thing, attacks every thing that comes in his way, and thinks himself the happiest and noblest being in the world. These men have kindly feelings. I should expect to receive more sympathy from them in real distress, such as they could understand, than from more enlightened, and more civilized men. They never swear. Their women never sit at table with them; at least, I have never seen them. I cannot speak in high terms of the manners or of the virtue of their squaws and daughters. Their houses contain but one room, and that used as a sleeping room as well by strangers as by the men of the family, they lose all feminine delicacy, and hold their virtue cheap.

XII

Dimensions of the Ohio — Its scenery — Velocity of the current — La Salle on the Ohio — Early settlements in the West — Struggle of frontiersmen and Indians — Population of the western states — The growth of Cincinnati — Description of the city — Manners of the people — The negro population — Story of the negro Anthony — Character of the flatboatmen.

Cincinnati March 6. 1818.

I wish you could see this town,[1] one of the most prosperous in the west. I will give you a sketch of it, its situation, and its early settlement.

---

[1] The site of Cincinnati was first occupied in 1780 when George Rogers Clark, in the course of his campaign against the allied British and Indian invaders of Ohio, gathered there about a thousand riflemen and built a blockhouse. In 1787, after the organization of the Northwest Territory, Judge John Cleves Symmes of New Jersey applied to Congress for a grant of a million acres of land lying north of the Ohio and between the Great and Little Miami rivers. The grant was obtained, though the tract was found eventually to contain not more than 600,000 acres, and in 1788 Symmes removed thither with his family and about fifty associates. His settlement was established on a site opposite the mouth of the Licking, receiving, at the suggestion of the Kentucky schoolmaster John Filson, the awkward name Lostantiville — the town (*ville*) opposite (*anti*) the mouth (*os*) of the Licking (*L*). When St. Clair, governor of the Northwest Territory, arrived in 1790 he very sensibly ruled that the town should be called Cincinnati, in honor of the military society of that name. Symmes was one of the first three judges associated with St. Clair in the management of Northwestern affairs. Cincinnati grew slowly at first, being for some time considerably more important as a stockade than as a town. In 1792 its first school and church were built and by 1800 it had a population of about seven hundred and fifty. It was the seat of government of the new state of Ohio until 1806, when the capital was transferred to Chillicothe. The census of 1810 gave it a population of 2,320, and in the following year Melish describes it as, next to Pittsburg, the greatest manufacturing town on the Ohio and a place rapidly increasing in size and advantages (*Travels,* ii, pp. 126-131). Its growth after this time was rapid, as is indicated by the fact that its population in 1813 was 4,000; in 1815, 6,000; in 1819, 10,283; and in 1826, 16,230. Travellers in the period 1816-1830 were generally surprised by the industrial and commercial activity of the place, as well as by the high state of society in it. The following visitors have good descriptions of the town: Fearon, *Sketches,* pp. 226-237;

12

The Ohio river is 1,000 miles long; join it with
the Alleghany it is 1,300. Its width at Cincinnati,
which is nearly equidistant from Pittsburgh and
its confluence with the Mississippi, is 534 yards;
which may be assumed, says D[r]. Drake,[1] as its
mean breadth. He is wrong;—I have gone down
900 miles, and have made by estimated angles above
50 measurements, and its average breadth cannot

Birkbeck, *Notes,* pp. 81-89; Hulme, *Journal* (EARLY WESTERN
TRAVELS, x, pp. 41-42); Nuttall, *Journal* (EARLY WESTERN TRAVELS,
xiii, p. 62); Flint, *Letters* (EARLY WESTERN TRAVELS, ix, pp. 149-
156); William Tell Harris, *Remarks,* p. 99; Woods, *Two Years'
Residence* (EARLY WESTERN TRAVELS, x, pp. 235-237); and Ogden,
Letters (EARLY WESTERN TRAVELS, xix, pp. 35-38). A very valuable
work on early Cincinnati is Daniel Drake's *Natural and Statistical
View or Picture of Cincinnati and the Miami Country* (Cincinnati,
1815), for which see note 1, below. Two very good popular
accounts are Francis W. Miller's *Cincinnati's Beginnings* (Cincinnati, 1880) and Ford and Ford, *History of Cincinnati* (Cincinnati,
1881).

[1] Daniel Drake was born in Kentucky in 1785. At the age of
fifteen he became a student of medicine at Cincinnati, where he
settled permanently in the practice of his chosen profession in 1807,
soon becoming one of the foremost physicians of the West. He established the Medical College of Ohio at Cincinnati (opened in
1820) and in 1827 was selected to be editor of the *Western Medical
and Physical Journal.* In 1810 he published a pamphlet entitled
Notices concerning Cincinnati, which constitutes the first authoritative description of the place of any length that we have. Five years
later his larger work, the *Natural and Statistical View or Picture of
Cincinnati and the Miami Country,* appeared — a book which served
a very useful purpose in promoting the prosperity of the city and
region described in it. It is this volume (pp. 13-17) that contains
the statements regarding the Ohio to which Fordham takes exception. Drake also published *History, Character, and Prospects of
the West: a Discourse* (Cincinnati, 1834); and by all odds his
greatest work was *On the Principal Diseases of the Interior Valley of North America,* published in 1850, two years before the
author's death. Further information will be found in Charles D.
Drake [ed.], *Pioneer Life in Kentucky: a Series of Reminiscential
Letters from Daniel Drake, M.D., of Cincinnati to his Children*
(Cincinnati, 1870); Charles D. Meigs, *A Biographical Notice of
Daniel Drake, M.D., of Cincinnati* (Philadelphia, 1853); and Edward Deering Mansfield, *Memoirs of the Life and Services of Daniel
Drake, with Notices of the Early Settlement of Cincinnati and
some of its Pioneer Citizens* (Cincinnati, 1855).

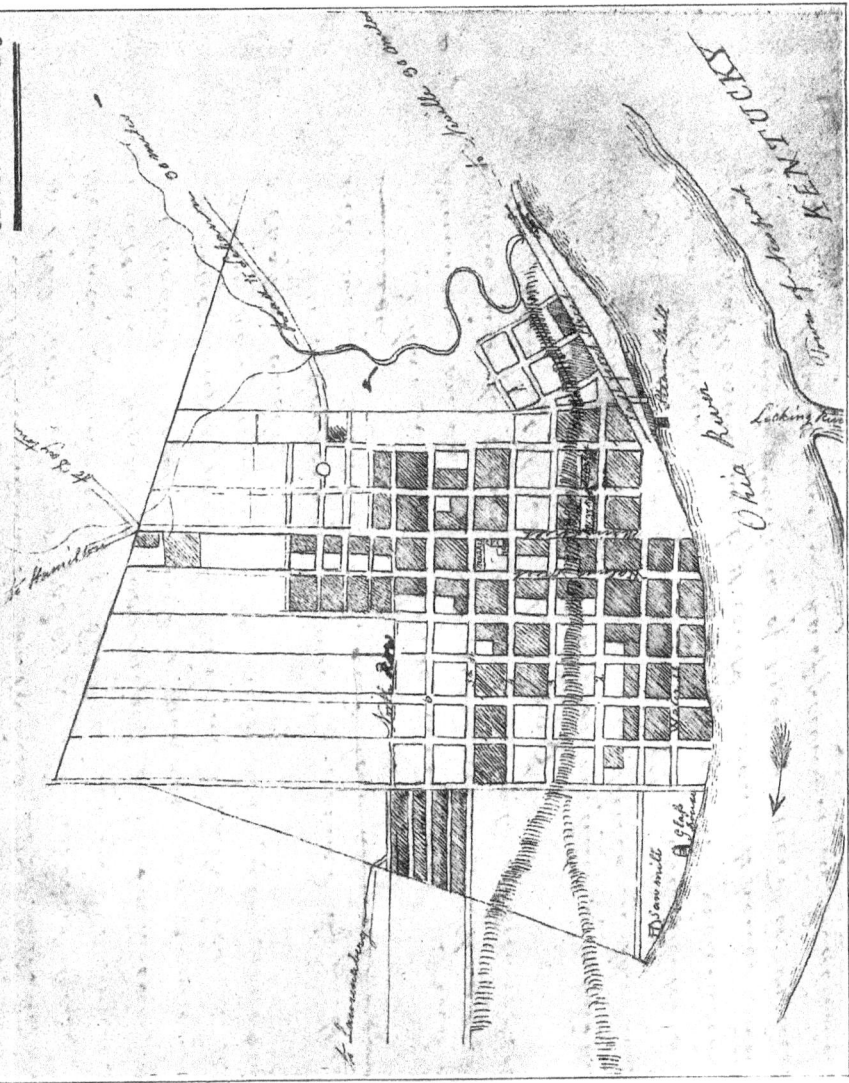

PLAN OF CINCINNATI.

be less than 700 yards. Its annual range from high to low water is 50 feet—its extreme range 7 feet more. It may be forded in many places above Louisville when the water is at the lowest stage; but between these bars, which form slight rapids, there are basins of deep water many miles long. It is frozen over at Pittsburg almost every winter—sometimes at Cincinnati—I believe never at Shawanoe. Generally navigation is stopt by floating ice 8 or 10 weeks.

The Ohio river is not generally a picturesque object. It addresses itself powerfully to the imagination, but not to the senses. Its banks are clothed with dark forests. Here and there a small cabin peeps from the trees. Sometimes the rocks rise around you in solemnity and gloom—but at one place only, at the falls, do your eyes glance over any expanse of country.

Nevertheless, I am more happy, more self-satisfied, on the banks of the Ohio, than ever I could have been on the fair plains of Old England. The forests of Indiana, the mountains of Kentucky, the wilds of the Illinois, if they are not so beautiful, yet their grandeur calls forth deeper, more sublime, emotions. They are the fields of enterprise, the cradle of freedom, the land of rest to the weary, the place of refuge to the oppressed. Every sound that issues from the woods, from the crashing tornado which rushes across entire regions, clothed in sheets of fire and shaking the hills to their foundations,—to the soft low murmur of an autumnal breeze, — all excites the most profound sentiments of adoration for the divine author of Nature, — all recall to man the uncertain duration of his existence; but these thoughts are unmixed with aught that can debase his worth or circumscribe his powers. These wildernesses are given to him alone: in them he is free; owning no master but his God, and no authority but that of reason and truth.

> "And sovereign man scarce condescends to see
> "A nation's laws more sovereign still than he."

To go back to the Ohio River. The velocity of its current is estimated at 3 miles per hour. When the waters are high and rising, it is equal to 4 and 5. But the progress of a boat must be estimated at less, because the filament of the current always inclines towards, and is generally very near, the concave shore; thus making the course of a boat longer than the length of the middle of the river: And there is generally a light breeze on the surface of the water, blowing upwards against it.

Monsr. de la Salle, a frenchman, in an inland voyage from Quebec to the Mississippi in 1680, descended the Ohio. Probably he was the first white man who ever navigated it; and his adventure was imitated by his countrymen exclusively for 70 years.[1] Vincennes, on the Wabash was founded

[1] On the achievements of La Salle, Fordham is badly confused. If La Salle ever descended the Ohio at all it must have been in 1670 or 1671. The claim is made, on the basis mainly of some questionable documents in Margry's *Découvertes et Etablissements des Français dans l'Ouest et dans le Sud de l'Amérique Septentrionale*, i, pp. 103-166, that the noted explorer, in the course of a western expedition from La Chine in 1670 discovered the Ohio and, following its course to the Mississippi, became also the French

in 1735;[1] and in 1753 Fort DuQuesne, at the confluence of the Monongahela and Alleghany.[2] In 1788, the first settlement was made in the State of Ohio, at Marietta by New Englanders.[3] In the autumn of the same year, a party of New Jersey men settled at the North Bend, just above the mouth of the Great Miami;[4] Fort Washington was built opposite the mouth of Licking, where Cincinnati now stands;[5] and the settlement of Columbia, just below the Little Miami, was undertaken.[6]

A dreadful War was waged by the Indians against the New Comers, who appear to have been well furnished with arms, and with nothing else. They used to steal out singly at night, and watch the deer come to the creeks to drink; and when

---

discoverer of this latter river. It is possible, as Parkman thought, that the Ohio was reached at this time and descended perhaps as far as to the site of Louisville, but that this was the case cannot be proved; that in any event no more than this was accomplished is practically beyond dispute. La Salle's expedition to the Mississippi in 1680 was made by way of the Great Lakes and the Illinois River.

[1] See p. 96, note 2.

[2] See p. 71, note. The date should be 1754.

[3] See p. 86, note.

[4] The town at North Bend, some miles west of Cincinnati, was established by Judge John Cleves Symmes in the hope that eventually it would be made the capital of the Northwest Territory. See p. 183, note.

[5] Fort Washington was established by Major Doughty in 1787 as a frontier protection against the Indians. Being no longer needed, it was demolished in 1808. Its site is marked at present by Fort Washington Monument, in Third Street, erected in 1901. See Robert Ralston Jones, *Fort Washington at Cincinnati, Ohio* (Cincinnati, 1902).

[6] In 1787 a block-house was built on the site of Columbia by Major Stiles, of Brownsville, Pennsylvania, and twenty-five associates. Like the slightly later settlement at North Bend (see note 4, above), Columbia was for a time a rival of Cincinnati for the dignity of capital of the Northwest Territory.

they had shot one, they were obliged to lie hid for some time to discover if any Indians were roused by the report of the gun; then the poor hunter would take the whole carcase on his back, and carry it perhaps 5 and 6 miles. They had seldom any bread, and sometimes no salt to eat with their Venison. In process of time they drove back the Indians, built their huts, made themselves farms, and married. Their children grew hardy and chubby by paddling in the mud, rolling in the sand, and eating hominy.

I copy the following table from D^r. Drake's book.[1]

Tenessee   settled in 1775 had in 1791 . . . . in 1800 . in 1810
                                    35691 inhabitants 105602 261727
Kentucky   settled in 1775 . . 1790 . . . . in 1800. in 1810
                                    73677 inh.   220690 406511
Ohio settled in 1788 . . . . . 1790 . . . . . 1800 . . 1810
                                    3000 inh.   42156 230670

		North'n States 100 to 101
The proportion of males to females...	Ohio 100 to 86 / Kentucky 100 to 91 / in Tenessee 100 to 93 in / Mexico 100 to 95 / Rhode Isl'd 100 to 105	Middle States 100 to 95 / South'n States 100 to 95

I shall tire you with dates and numbers. Let us see what Cincinnati is now. It stands on the first and second banks of the Ohio. The second is 40 feet higher than the first. The two banks are both plains nearly parallel with the horizon. At the distance of a mile from the river you come to steep hills above 300 feet high.

In 1810 Cincinnati contained 2,320 Inhabitants;

[1] Daniel Drake, *Natural and Statistical View of Cincinnati*, p. 28. See *ante*, p. 184, note.

in 1814, 4,000, in 1815, 6,000; at the present time the lowest estimation is 8,000, living in 800 houses. There are 6 places of worship; 2 presbyterian, 2 methodist, 1 baptist and 1 quaker; no Roman Catholic Chapel, though there are Catholics; a unitarian has preached here, and they talk of getting a Chapel built.

It is a Corporation town, governed by a Mayor, and twelve councilmen.

It has a Court house and gaol, a public seminary on Lancaster's plan, and a Theatre fallen into disrepute, and in a state of dilapidation. The Steam Mill cost 130,000$.

M^r. Greene's foundery is a flourishing establishment. He has workmen equal to do any thing in Machinery.

There are four Banks. They issue notes as low as dollars. There are tickets in circulation of as small value as 6¼ Cents — about 4 pence. This is the smallest division of money, and is valued about as much as a halfpenny is in England.

There is a United States' Land Office here, and M^r. Jesse Embree has established a Land agency office, at which emigrants may procure information, that might otherwise cost them many hundred miles travelling to obtain.

The houses of the principal streets are built of brick, and are handsome without and convenient within. The upper part of the Town is not yet much built upon, and is chiefly encumbered by mean paltry wooden houses; though there are some dwellings with their proud porticos, that look too aristocratic by half for the State of Ohio. Around the town are scattered a few good and many indifferent villas and ornamented Cottages; like, but unequal to those near London.

The river, which is now rising, and open, displays a gay and busy scene. Boats and barges, some of which are schooner-rigged, are taking in or discharging cargoes. Flour is shipped here, which you possibly may eat in London, and English goods block up the path along the shore. Some of these boats are manned by Sailors, and their cheerful shouts and *yo-hoing* make me forget I am 1,500 miles from the Ocean.

Of the manners of the Citizens of Cincinnati I ought to say but little, for my acquaintance has been confined to the Quakers. Servants are so difficult to be obtained that the wives and daughters of the middle classes do nearly all the household work themselves, and a negro, unless you hire him by the month to clean your boots will charge you each time 12½ Cents. This, however, is not the case with the very rich, who live in plenty and even splendour, that would excite the envy of an English Shopkeeper. There are several carriages and some one-horse chaises, but Jersey waggons are more common and more useful.

The western Americans are not so domestic as the English. Business and politics engross the thoughts of the men. They live in their Stores and Counting houses, and associate with their wives as little as may be. The latter are generally inferior in information and talents of conversation to English women of the same station in life. They are good managers in their houses, but are fond of dress, in which they have but little taste. The Ohio women are pretty, but not interesting. We sometimes meet with one who is above the common standard, but she is, ten to one, an Emigrant from the East.

But, however, there is no standard of manners, no classification of these people, who have come perhaps from the Mountains of Vermont or the barren sands of Nantucket, from Massachusetts and Connecticut and from every State in the Union, from the frozen regions of Canada, from every Country in Europe.

There are a few white servants, chiefly indentured girls, who are allowed indulgencies which would astonish an English housekeeper. They are treated rather as poor relations, or as children, than as menials. Black servants will take liberties that are not granted.

There are a few Negroes here; perhaps 200 in the whole town. More dissipated, vile, insolent beings there cannot be. I have been on the point of knocking my Shoeblack down twice. I changed him;—and but little for the better. It will not do to speak to a Negro as you must to a white man; he assumes upon it immediately. Yet I know Negroes who are most excellent servants. M^r. J——
has one—his story is worth relating.

Anthony was brought into Indiana by a man named Hopkins, who became Sheriff, and went with the Militia to Tippecanoe. He took Anthony with him as a waggoner. In that fiercely fought battle the Americans nearly yielded to the onset of the Indians. Anthony, who was safe amidst the baggage, rushed into the thickest of the fight, snatched a rifle from a dying soldier, and fought by the side of his Master. When Indiana became a state, slavery was abolished and Anthony was free.[1] He said to his Master, "You bought me but a little while ago for a great deal of money; you will lose it, if I leave you now. I will indenture myself for 10 years." His offer was accepted by Hopkins, who afterwards *sold him as a slave for life* to some Orleans traders, who wanted to take him by force down to Louisiana, where he would have been worked, starved, and flogged into feebleness and submission. Anthony, who is as strong as an Ath-

---

[1] The provision of the Ordinance of 1787 that there should be "neither slavery nor involuntary servitude" in the Northwest Territory was understood by the people of the Territory to mean simply that free negroes could not legally be enslaved and that slaves could not be brought in from outside sources. It was assumed that the ordinance was not retroactive and did not affect the status of slaves already held at the time of its promulgation; and this assumption was proved well founded when the question was tested subsequently in the courts. The population of southern Indiana and Illinois was largely of southern origin. It included many residents who were slave-holders in 1787 and many others who came in after that date, bringing their slaves with them and holding them on sufferance. An elaborate system of indented servitude also prevailed, and it was not until the adoption of the constitution of the state of Indiana in 1816 that slavery, or its practical equivalent, was finally and absolutely abolished in that portion of the old Territory. On the great struggle over slavery which went on in Indiana during the period 1800-1812 see John D. Dillon, *History of Indiana*, chapter xxxi, and Jacob P. Dunn, *Indiana*, chapter vi.

lete, broke from them and ran into Princeton, where his part was taken by my friend M^r. J——, who bought his time and treats him as a friend rather than a servant. In three years he will be free, and he talks of going to his father, who lives among the Chickasaws, but I tell him I shall want him. As I always pay him the respect due to his virtues and almost heroic character, he is very much attached to me. He is learning to read of M^r. Birkbeck's servant.

This man Anthony is as well made as any white. His colour is deep black. There is a quickness and cheerfulness about him, which makes him an excellent servant.

The whites here hold themselves above the blacks, be they bondsmen or free. The blacks are the Helots of this modern Sparta.

Workmen of every class are upon an equality with every man. I am now surrounded by those of M^r. Green's Shops, whose address is equal to that of many an Englishman who farms his thousand acres; they expect civility and they generally return it.

The boatmen who used to be my aversion, are not nearly so much so now. There are some incorrigible scoundrels among them; and their conversation and manners are only to be equalled in the sinks of London; but should you take a respectable young woman on board a boat, especially if it be your own, you will not hear a word to offend you. — But I would advise all travellers going alone down the river, to get one man at least that they can depend upon, and to wear a dagger or a brace of pistols; for there are no desperadoes more savage in their anger than these men. Give them your hand, — accost them with a bold air, — taste their whisky, — and you win their hearts. But a little too much reserve or haughtiness offends them instantly, and draws upon you torrents of abuse, if not a personal assault. They are a dauntless, hardy set; thoughtless, and short lived from intemperance. I must say for them, that, since I have understood their characters, I have never received a saucy word from any of them.

I write in a desultory manner, which I hope you will excuse; and I hope you will never imagine things to be worse than I represent them. I give the darker shade to every vice, the full, broad, outline to all I dislike in this Country. So pray do not let your imagination dwell on the ills, which follow the footsteps of man wherever he goes.

The family I am in are from Nantucket. In the Pennsylvanian farmer's letter by Hector S^t. John, there is a pretty description of that little island, and it is correct, I am told, in all respects, but one in which he mentions the general use of opium.[1]

The Nantucketers are most like the good, old fashioned English, of any Americans I have seen. To me, now I am becoming an American, they seem to be absolutely English. Perhaps there may be

---

[1] Two more recent descriptions of the island are R. H. Cook's *Historical Notes on the Island of Nantucket* (Nantucket, 1871) and William R. Bliss's *Quaint Nantucket* (Boston, 1896).

some differences, but they are not very obvious. I am treated by this family with great kindness, as much so as if I were a Son of it. I should say that part of the family is from New Jersey, who are next akin to English. New Yorkers, perhaps, come next.

XIII

English Prairie May 5. 1818.

I SHALL attend to your desire to have a meteorological diary kept: it is the only way of obtaining a correct knowledge of the temperature of the climate.

M^r. B. has noted in his almanack the variations of the Thermometer till he left Princeton 3 weeks ago. — I will give you now from memory a sketch of the changes since July 1817.

July.   Therm. at noon 75°. to 85°.—at night, perhaps, 50°. to 55°.—Thunderstorm once in 10 days—no fogs or hazy weather.

August.   75°. to 90°. Thunderstorms, frequent — clear weather and warm nights.

Sept^r.   70°. to 85°. Thunderstorms and hard rain two or three days, nights warm.

October.   40°. to 80°. Cold winds and rains the latter part of the month.

November.	40°. to 70°. A few days of hazy weather, succeeded by the Indian Summer, during which the sky was always obscured as if by smoke. The weather warm and pleasant. The sun looked red, and the clouds yellowish. This was succeeded by rain and after by cool weather — It was still pleasant sleeping in the woods.
December.	Therm: varied a good deal. Sometimes we sat out of doors in the evening. The month closed with hard frosts, which broke up after 10 days duration — say for this month —

1st. week 40°. to 55°. at noon.

2^{d}. —— 35°. to 50°.

3^{d}. —— at night 8°. below 0. at noon 10° and 15°. above.

4th. —— The frost broke up with cold rain.

January.	Pleasant weather; generally 50°. at noon.
February.	Freezing hard and thawing again. Weather changing every week.
March.	Cold winds, — quite English March weather.
April.	English April weather.
May. 5th.	Trees are putting forth leaves, grass beginning to grow, and woods gay with blossoms.

The oldest Indian traders say that there has been more rain, and that it has been altogether severer, this winter, than they have known for thirty years. Some very old men say at the first settling of S^t. Vincennes 60 years ago, there were two or three such winters. Much credit cannot be given to such long recollections. The waters of the Wabash this winter rose to some very old water marks, which evidently had not been touched for many years.

When the Thermometer is 10°. below Zero, it is impossible to warm a boarded frame house. A good log or plastered one may be made warm. Men never think of working in this weather, but every body crowds round the tavern fires to talk politics. The bear hunters, however, choose this weather, and go out 9 or 10 days without returning home. They make blanket tents, open towards the fire, which is an oblong pyramid of logs 10 feet by 3 or 4 at the base.

The coldest weather is cheerful: fogs are almost unknown, except on large bodies of water. On the Ohio I have known it so dark at 10 a. m. that I could not see 30 yards.

This spring is later than any ever remembered. There is, upon the whole, a superiority in the Climate of the western Country to that of England; though not so great as I at first imagined, or as you would expect from the latitude. Consumptions are almost unknown here. Bilious fevers are rather prevalent, but not dangerous when early attended to. Women have not such good health as the men have; but that is to be attributed to their mode of life, — being always in the house, usually without shoes and stockings, and roasting themselves over large fires.

People are not so long-lived here as in England, and they look old sooner. This I think may be justly attributed to

1ˢᵗ. The universal use of spirituous liquors.

2ᵈˡʸ. The disregard of personal comfort and cleanliness, exposure to bad air near swamps &c, and want of good Clothing.

3ᵈˡʸ. The great stimulus and excitement of the mental passions, which adventurers and first settlers are, by their situation, subject to.

4ᵗʰˡʸ. (Perhaps) violent religious enthusiasm.

5ᵗʰˡʸ. In some instances, very early marriages.

I find it no easy task to write descriptions of manners and opinions. If individual pictures only be drawn, the inferences must be in part erroneous; and sketches of a more comprehensive nature are either loose and incorrect, or tame and unreadable.

Harmonie on the Wabash — May 6.

Robert W—— arrived at Princeton on Sunday, while I was taking a walk in the woods with Mʳ. S——. As we returned into the town, a woman poked her head out of a hole, called a window, in the side of a log cabin, and screamed out "An Englishman is come."

I ran home, and found whole packets of letters. *You do not know* what it is to have letters from a long left native land.—I did not sleep that night.

The next morning Robert and I started for the Prairie. I took him the shortest road, or rather through Woods and Swamps where there was no road at all. He had been wearied by his journey and discouraged. I talked, laughed, galloped and splashed along, to his great astonishment, who could not imagine that a civilized Englishman could like such a dismal Country.

We came to the Wabash: Even "the handsome river," with its silver waves, excited in the Londoner no admiration. At Coffee Settlement[1] there was daylight, but no inhabitants but Canadian French and Creoles.[2]

Eight miles more of woods and wet prairies brought us to Bonpas, and my friends the W——'s, fine specimens of backwoodsmen. Their hospitable, not to say, courteous manners, frank and intrepid look, and the pleasure they expressed at seeing me, pleased Robert: here he felt a little better.

We then travelled through some rough, brushy woods, broken by ravines; then through part of the Long Prairie and a narrow strip of wood; and the *English Prairie,* with all its swelling hills, meandering brooks, and dark surrounding forests, opened at once upon our sight. A strong North-

---

[1] Coffee Creek is a little stream flowing into the Wabash six miles below Mount Carmel, in Wabash County, Illinois. The settlement to which Fordham refers was on this creek, eight miles from Bonpas. See p. 118, note 2.—EDITOR.

This word is pronounced in the back woods "saitelmeant."

—FORDHAM.

[2] Half or quarter bred Indians.—FORDHAM.

westerly wind swept off the clouds over the Southern ridges, and the sun shone forth in the clear sky of a Southern climate, throwing alternate light and shade on the wood-clothed hills, which rise above each other in long succession till they are lost in the blue horizon. Robert exclaimed, "This is grand!" and I was shaking hands with him to welcome him to *our territory*, when four deer springing from a thicket startled our horses; and his ran away with him across the Prairie. We reached the settlement at sun down; and that night Robert shared my blanket on the floor of a new Cabin.

Yesterday I left the English Prairie with ——, and came here to engage hands to take a keel boat to Shawnee. I must go then to enter land, and shall return immediately on horseback to superintend the building of houses to receive ——'s and my people. Mine will be French Canadians.

I have hired one man, his wife and three boys, great and small, for 15$ per month, and I am to find them food. The woman is to cook and wash for me. DuG—— has offered me his eldest son, 15 years old, a very nice boy, on trial. I have sent to Vincennes for 3 more men; besides which I want to contract with Americans to build four houses, and to make two miles of fence railing, and one mile of ditching.

I have surveyed the land next behind mine, and only one quarter section is good. There are some hills of thin timber, such as will lie unoccupied, perhaps five or six years. But I think I can find some good land for you near the Brushy Prairie. The English Prairie is entirely taken up by our party, except 3 quarter sections at the bottom, which I have no doubt will be bought by some of us.

I shall enter one quarter more north of my own, which will make my farm 480 acres, of which 200 acres will be good prairie, and the remaining 280 acres, white oak, post oak, shell-bark hickory and walnut land, that is pretty good second rate land, such as will grow fine wheat crops, and about 50 bushels of Maize per acre. The timber is very thrifty, apparently of about 40 or 50 years growth.

I will not enter inferior land for you for the sake of proximity. The country is filling up fast; so it will answer better to buy good land further off.

I am obliged to you for remembering me. I can assure you, I often think of you in this land of dirt, bad cooking, and discomfort of every kind.

But I am not, thanks to the very nice family I am with, either discouraged, or yet quite a hottentot. I still prefer sweet butter to grease, milk fresh from the cow to sour and rancid swill; although, I like corn or hoe cakes, hominy (that is boiled corn) and mush (hasty pudding made of Indian meal) and stewed pumpkins very well. I change my shirt, when it is convenient, twice a week, and sometimes take my clothes off when I go to bed. My hands, though rougher by far, are not quite so dark as an Indian's; and moreover I am grown very stout.

M[r]. Birkbeck does not mean to introduce more American customs in our Colony than will be necessary. English ideas and manners will be preserved as much as possible; and already we begin to be respected. Some of the wildest fellows want to remove, but other respectable men wish to get near us. So in many respects the desert will soon begin to smile.

When we first came out there was no population to withstand an incursion of Indians, if a war had been excited by the violent and cruel hunters. Our houses were planned to be easily converted into forts, and bastions erected at the angles. These precautions will be unnecessary now; though M[r]. B., who never pronounces the word fear, and Judge H., a cidevant Soldier, both thought them to be prudential measures a few months ago.

However, should a war break out on our frontiers, I hope there is not nor will be, a young Englishman among us, who would hesitate to turn out with his gun and blanket. There is much less Indian Territory in Illinois than in Indiana.

I am at Harmonie,[1] where I am now well ac-

---

[1] The town of Harmony, properly New Harmony, in Posey County, Indiana, was established in 1815 by a company of Germans under the leadership of George Rapp. The settlement, which was one of the most unique in the history of the West, was the ultimate outgrowth of a migration from the German state of Württemberg a decade earlier. In Württemberg at the beginning of the century the Lutheran creed was being imposed relentlessly upon all the inhabitants and it was felt by many that the principles of religion were being employed by the government merely as convenient tools of despotism. One man of influence holding this opinion was George Rapp (1757-1847) who proceeded to get together at Iptingen a group of persons of similar mind and to form them into a society to live after what he conceived to be the ideal plan of the New

quainted both with the leaders Messrs. Rapp Senr. and Junr. and with the people. I am treated here with great kindness.

Their monastic way of life *is*, which I once doubted, the result of religious conviction. I have talked with some of them on their religious Principles. The Tavern is conducted in the most orderly and cleanly manner that a tavern can be in America, where men spit *every where*, and, almost on *every thing*. Now they know my habits are European, they put me in a clean bed, give me clean towels, and pay me more respect than they do any American.

Testament. The speedy incurring of fines and imprisonment at the hands of the authorities prompted Rapp and his associates to decide to emigrate to the United States. In 1803 Rapp and a few companions came out as agents of the society to select a site for the future settlement. The location chosen was on Conequenessing Creek, in Butler County, Pennsylvania, about thirty miles northwest of Pittsburg. In 1804 the society embarked at Amsterdam and in the following year a town was laid out on the proposed site and given the name Harmony. Within twelve months the colony had come to comprise ninety families. A tract of nine thousand acres was bought, mills and factories were erected, and the thrift and frugality of the settlers soon brought material prosperity. In 1811 the society had eight hundred members. In the course of a few years the region around Harmony became so thickly settled that land rose to a high value and the Germans saw an opportunity to increase their capital by selling their original tract and moving to another farther West. In 1813 Rapp purchased for the use of his colony thirty thousand acres in the south-western corner of Indiana and there, two years later, the town of New Harmony was laid out. In 1824 this location was purchased in turn by George Flower for Robert Owen, of New Lanark, Scotland, who desired to use it in experimenting with his communistic projects. The year following Rapp led his colony back to Pennsylvania and settled it in the new town of Economy, in Beaver County, seventeen miles northwest of Pittsburg. After some years of interesting but on the whole not encouraging efforts at New Harmony, Owen gave up his enterprise and returned to Scotland. Because of its location and its unique character the New Harmony settlement, especially under Rapp's occupancy, was visited by virtually every traveller who came at all near it and as a consequence a number of valuable descriptions were

Their cooking, their dress, is exactly the same as it was on the banks of the Rhine. Their language is German. They are orderly, civil people, and their town is already very neat. The houses, log-built, are placed at regular distances, and are each surrounded by a neat kitchen and flower garden, paled in. The footpath is divided from the road by rows of lombardy poplars. M^r. Rapp's house is a handsome brick building, by far the best in Indiana.

The Harmonists have, to each family a cow, which comes to its owner's gate every morning and evening. In the woods they are kept by herdsmen. They have public ovens, public stores, and every thing in common. They brew beer and make wine: the latter is kept for the sick and to sell. They all dress alike: — M^r. Rapp as the meanest labourer; — except when he goes out of town.

They are great musicians, and many of them study music as a Science. Once a week they have a concert at M^r. Rapp's, to which I am invited.

Their church is a neat wooden building, painted white. It has a tower, a bell, and a clock. The

left on record, such as that which Fordham here gives. Other contemporary accounts are Birkbeck, *Notes,* pp. 135-142; Hulme, *Journal* (EARLY WESTERN TRAVELS, x, pp. 53-61) ; Bradbury, *Travels* (EARLY WESTERN TRAVELS, v, pp. 314-316) ; Woods, *Two Years' Residence* (EARLY WESTERN TRAVELS, x, pp. 312-315) ; Welby, *Visit to North America* (EARLY WESTERN TRAVELS, xii, p. 260, ff.) ; and Faux, *Memorable Days* (EARLY WESTERN TRAVELS, xi, p. 248, ff.). George B. Lockwood's *The New Harmony Communities* (Marion, Indiana, 1902) is the best general history of the Rapp settlement, though Hinds, *American Communities* (Chicago, 1902) contains a fair account. For the history of the Rappites themselves Sachse's *German Sectarians of Pennsylvania* (Philadelphia, 1900) is useful.

men sit at one end of the church and the women at the other; and M^r. Rapp sits while he preaches in a chair placed on a stage, about one yard high, with a table before him. When I heard him one week day evening, he wore a linsey woolsey coat and a blue worsted night cap. In praying the Harmonists do not rise up nor kneel down, but bend their bodies forward, almost to their knees. Their singing is very good.

The country people hate the Harmonists very much, because they permit no drunkenness in their taverns.

When I make severe remarks on the Americans, you must understand I always except a considerable number; some of whom would be ornaments to any Country. Judge H——, S——, and B—— (though quite a youth) are of this number. . . .

XIV

Rise of land values — The question of admitting slavery — Lack of
free laborers — Wages and expenses of laborers — Land for
every immigrant — Mr. Birkbeck's plan for the settlement of
his English laborers — Difficulties of establishing a settlement
— Threatened incursion of Indians — Kentucky hospitality —
Mode of life of the Kentuckians.

Princeton June 20. 1818.

KENTUCKIAN Speculators are very busy in every
direction around us, and I expect that land on the
Wabash, the Ohio, the Illinois, and the Mississippi,
will be very shortly worth from 5$ to 30$ per acre.
Perhaps in two or three years; and as far inland as
the beneficial effects of navigation can be felt. The
rise of the value of land will be modified by the circumstances of local situation, quantity and quality
of timber, water, and, — more than all, — by the decision of the Convention, now about to be elected,
upon the grand question of Slavery.[1] If Slavery
be admitted, it is the opinion of many that well-

---

[1] The constitution framed by the convention of 1818 and subsequently adopted contained a provision (Art. VI, §1) which was
interpreted as prohibiting the further introduction of slaves into the
new state but not as liberating those already held there or abolish-
ing slavery as an institution. These latter ends were not achieved
until the second constitution was adopted in 1848. The census of
1820 showed that Illinois contained 917 slaves, and that of 1830,
746. The years 1822-1825 were marked by a bitter struggle between
the pro-slave and free-state elements, resulting from an attempt to
change the constitution so that it would give positive rather than
mere negative protection to slavery. The leader of the free-state
party was Edward Coles, who had been elected governor of the
commonwealth in August, 1822. Coles was a Virginian and had
been a slave-holder, but he was strongly opposed to the conversion
of nominally free into avowedly slave soil. In the fight which he
waged with the pro-slave party after his election his most active
supporters were the inhabitants of the English Settlement in Edwards County, notably Morris Birkbeck, George and Richard Flower,

chosen land will double in value in one day; and no good and well-situated land will be worth less than 10$ per acre. In fact, some land is worth 10$ per acre at this moment, and a section at the mouth of Bon pas is valued by the owner at 15$ per acre. I believe M^r. B. will purchase it.

I would not have upon my conscience the moral guilt of extending Slavery over countries now free from it, for the whole North Western Territory. But, if it should take place, I do not see why I should not make use of it. If I do not have servants I cannot farm; and there are *no* free labourers here, except a few so worthless, and yet so haughty, that an English Gentleman can do nothing with them.

A man used to work will earn in one day what will suffice for the simple wants of a Backwoodsman a whole week. If he be sober and industrious, in two years he can enter a quarter section of land, buy a horse, a plough, and tools. The lowest price for labour now is 13$ per month with board and

and Gilbert Pell; and that the balance was finally turned in favor of freedom and against slavery was due in no small measure to the efforts of these men. Birkbeck, in fact, was Coles's main reliance in the southern, pro-slave section of the state. In October, 1824, when David Blackwell, Secretary of State, resigned his office, Coles gave the place to Birkbeck in recognition of his services and his fitness for it. The nomination required confirmation by the Senate, however, and that body, having a pro-slave majority, voted on January 15, 1825, to reject the appointee. Birkbeck was thus forced to retire after having served three months. On the slavery struggle of this period see William H. Brown, *An Historical Sketch of the Early Movement in Illinois for the Legalization of Slavery* (Chicago, 1865); Elihu B. Washburne, *Sketch of Edward Coles, second governor of Illinois, and of the Slavery Struggle of 1823-4* (Chicago, 1882); and George Flower, *History of the English Settlement in Edwards County, Illinois* (Chicago, 1882).

lodging. I will give two years net proceeds in figures.

	$		$
12 months at 13$ . . .	156$	Clothing for two years —	
12 months at 13 . . .	156	say	100
	$312	One quarter of land . . .	80
		One horse and harness and plough	100
		Axe grubbing hoe &c . .	10
		Gun and powder &c . . .	15
			$305

After putting in his crop of maize, he can supply himself with meat and some money by hunting, or he can earn $1 per day in splitting rails for his neighbours. Many men begin as independent farmers with half the above mentioned sum, but they are thorough Backwoodsmen.

Now, is it not evident that while land can be bought, no matter how far from navigable rivers, at $2 per acre, and when there are tracts they may "squat" upon for nothing, that labour will be for many years limited in price only by the ability of those who want it, to pay for it. It is indeed the only expence; but is so overwhelming that I would rather farm in old England with a capital of 2 or 3000£ than on the North West of the Ohio. If we consider the immense territory to the North West of us, and the roving spirit of the Americans, we may wonder that any work can be hired. The truth is, none are to be hired but Emigrants from the Eastern States, who intend to be land owners in one, two, or three years. And these are few in number: for the steady and prudent earn the money at home and bring it with them.

M^r. Birkbeck's object is to settle his old servants around him, and, while they earn money to enable them to be independent farmers, he will get his Estate greatly improved. It will be raised in value by the industrious population around improving the land he sells. Thus his speculation will succeed; and he will be gratified by his being looked up to as the chief of the Colony: but for immediate, or even distant, profit in money, he does not expect. His English labourers have already caught the desire to be land owners, but they rely on his promise to let them have land when they can pay for it at 2$ per acre. They feel gratified for this generosity, which is in fact a wise and liberal policy.

Our colony now contains between 40 and 50 persons, besides American settlers in the neighbourhood. M^r. B. with great difficulty gets Cabins erected by the Backwoodsmen; and not nearly fast enough for the demand. His own people finish them, make fences &c. I cannot convey to you any idea of the difficulties one meets with at every step in founding a colony; especially when food is to be carried on horses, or a waggon, and a road to be made 12 miles to a river, where it is to be unloaded from boats on to land the property of a stranger, and which is unsettled. Then every article must be slightly covered in a Camp, and guarded, or exposed to the cupidity of the boatmen or hunters. Horses are to be broken in to work together; waggons, carts, and ploughs to be made, or brought several days journey. Even when they are ordered, there is no certainty of the order being executed: for the Smith has no iron; you buy it, then he has no coal. The Wheelwright is gone a hunting, or is drunk, or attending a lawsuit. The Sadler and collar maker will sell the articles you have ordered to the first comer. — You are sure of nothing; not even when you go for it yourself; except at Harmonie where business is done, when they have time, with great regularity.

M^r. Birkbeck has fifty acres fenced. He has sunk two wells 20 or 30 feet, and found coal instead of water. He must try elsewhere. I have one cabin covered in, and one house of hewn logs nearly done for ——. There is a small spring near his house.

Some of M^r. Birkbeck's men are sick. I have all mine, except a frenchman, engaged by the job; and they are all well. I expect an additional force from Harmonie of 3 men and 2 women, just arrived from Switzerland. They are good looking people, and one speaks a little french.[1] . . .

A message from the prairie informs me, that 8 backwoodsmen are gone to drive off some Indians from a creek near my line. They have killed 20 does in one day. If the Indians resist they will be murdered.

---

[1] The most notable settlement of Swiss people in the West was that at Vevay, Indiana. In 1802 John James Du Four obtained from Congress a grant of two thousand five hundred acres of land on the Ohio for the purpose of establishing an experimental colony for the culture of the vine. A considerable number of settlers were brought over from the Swiss district of Vevay, and in 1813 the Indiana town of Vevay, in Switzerland County, was laid out. Descendants of these original settlers own most of the land about the town today. William Tell Harris, in 1817, gives a good characterization of the settlement (*Remarks*, pp. 126-127).

I have been here two days since my return from
Kentucky, ill from riding in the sun. But I shall
go to the Prairie tomorrow or Robert W. will be
uneasy. He lives in my cabin and takes care of
the provisions and stores. I shall put it into a de-
fensible state, if any mischief has been done; but I
shall be under no personal apprehensions; for besides being known to a great many Indians, I can
bring down deer, birds and squirrels at every shot
with my rifle. I have done harm to none, and I
have not the least fear that any will do harm to
me.

In my late visit to Kentucky I have become acquainted with several respectable families. M^r. A.
received us with great kindness and hospitality. I
will describe our reception, and it will answer for
all the rest of our visits. We alighted at the Inn at
Henderson[1] and sent for M^r. B——. M^r. A. came
with him and took us to his house, a neatly furnished cabin-built cottage. We then sent for our
horses. M^rs. A—— ordered a second dinner.
Toddy, ice and fruit were handed about. A foot-
man shewed me to my room, and then acted as valêt
de chambre.

---

[1] Henderson, as well as the county in which the town is situated,
took its name from Colonel Richard Henderson, a Virginian who
had an important part in the early settlement of Kentucky. It was
also known as Red Banks, and sometimes as Hendersonville.
Audubon, the famous naturalist, having failed as a merchant in
Louisville, took up his residence at Henderson in 1812, though he
did not become known to the outside world until fourteen or fifteen
years later. Woods (*Two Years' Residence*) records that in 1820
the town contained about a hundred dwellings, together with a
court-house, a jail, a steam mill, and several tobacco warehouses
(Early Western Travels, x, p. 252).

My dirty shirt, cravat, &c, was taken possession of by the laundress. At dinner, every thing in profusion; — but no imported luxuries. Ice was placed on the butter and on the water and in the water jug. Whisky and Toddy instead of Wine. Supper — much the same, with the addition of tea and coffee, — the only imported luxuries in the house; M^r. A.'s garden and icehouse furnished all the rest. My bed was delightfully adapted for a warm climate; sheets like gauze, and gauze mosquito curtains around it.

We visited Judge T——, M^r. H——, M^r. A——s and Gen. H——, members of Congress. Not one of these gentlemen live in so good a house as that of our baker at —— in England. Gen. H—— has 160 negroes, who live in cottages on the skirts of the farm of 500 acres, which is cut out of immense and dark forests. In the centre of this clearing are the old rotten cabins which are occupied by the General and his genteelly dressed daughters; to each of whom he gives 10 negroes and a farm, for a marriage portion.

Many gentlemen live just as well as the General, who have only 70 or 80 acres of productive land.

The Kentuckians are so hospitable that they will stop you on the road, and oblige you to go to their houses, if they have ever seen you in respectable society.

This has happened to me, and I have not been suffered to pursue my journey till I had promised to call again and sleep.

Though the houses near Henderson are bad, there are good gardens and icehouses; and cleanliness, which strongly contrasts with the dirty Ohio houses, and the Indiana and Illinois pigsties, in which men women and children wallow in promiscuous filth. But the Kentuckians have servants; and whatever may be the future consequences of Slavery, the present effects are in these respects most agreeable and beneficial. A Kentuckian farmer has the manners of a gentleman; he is more or less refined according to his education, but there is generally a grave, severe, dignity of deportment in the men of middle age, which prepossesses, and commands respect. . . .

I thought I was Mosquito proof last year; but in sleeping at the mouth of the Bon pas 3 weeks ago, I was terribly bitten. I have been exposed to their attacks once since, and my body is covered with swellings, which itch intolerably. After the skin is once inoculated and saturated with the poison of these insects, their bites have but little effect. . . .

I am not at present very well. The weather is very hot. — Therm: 90°. — the sky clear: — if a cloud passes once a week, a thunder gust drives it off. We have had a slight shock of an Earthquake.

A Prussian Baron B——, who was five years Minister at the Court of Louis 15, is coming to visit me.

XV

Mr. Birkbeck's book — A journal of ten days — A fourth of July celebration — The ,coming struggle over slavery in Illinois — Acts of Congress regarding Illinois — A projected trip up the Red River — Character of the backwoodsman — High regard for Englishmen — The life of the hunters on the Wabash — The hunters on the Missouri — Men needed to develop the wilderness.

Princeton July 6ᵗʰ. 1818.

You have read Mʳ. Birkbeck's book.[1]— It is correct as far as it goes; but it is the sketch of a traveller, who tells the truth when he finds it. But, Truth, grotto loving Goddess, is not often to be seen, except by glimpses, by a Traveller. Mʳ. B. could now write a better book if he would; but, in describing this country, all he would say of the manners of the people, would be tinctured by his preconceived notions. Sketches in general have hitherto been too sunny.

I will give you my journal of the last ten days.

June 26ᵗʰ.—Went with Mʳ. R——, just arrived from England, to our settlement. Before we left Princeton filled our pockets with biscuits, and carried two sacks of corn (maize) for our horses. At Coffee Island Swamp Mʳ. R—— was astonished that I left the road and all visible track, to go through a part that was not so deep a bog. He offered me his compass, which I, a little vain of my hunting instincts, declined using. — We came out 2 miles from the place we entered exactly where the road passes between the two ponds.

---
[1] See p. 176, note.

14

27th. Hunting land with M[r]. R——. Did not find any that quite pleased us. Crossed the Piankeshaw Prairie at noon — Sun — burning hot. Reached M[r]. Q——'s Cabin just at dinner time — it is floored and carpetted. It is made of Hickory logs, and is ornamented with large mirrors in gilded frames, a handsome four post bedstead &c. It looked like a fairy bower in the wilderness.

28th. Started alone at daybreak from my own humble cabin and went to B—— of Burke's prairie.[1] Taking my departure from thence I plunged into the trackless woods, having my surveying compass and maps with me. Ran the lines through ——'s Prairie; and noted some fine land to be bought for him. Returned at night weary and hungry to Burke's Cabin; where I found nothing but a hearty welcome to corn cake and some sweet milk, which M[rs]. B—— said she had kept *sweet* because I liked it so, better than *sour*.

29th. B—— accompanied me to the Banks of the Little Wabash. He went fishing while I swam across the river. Not liking the growth of timber there, I returned, and he took me a few miles up the stream, to a rich bottom, where I took notes of 480 acres of land to be entered for my uncle K——. B—— shewed me this day how to entice does by bleating. But though he could bring the beautiful

[1] Properly, *Birks's* Prairie. This prairie was a long, narrow belt comprising about four thousand acres of excellent land and situated three miles west of the English Prairie. It took its name from its earliest resident, Jeremiah Birks, a Kentuckian who, after the influx of English settlers in the vicinity, moved on across the Mississippi.

affectionate looking creatures within twenty steps, and leveled his unerring rifle several times, he would not shoot one. Yet there was no meat in his cabin and we lived this day on squirrels. We saw fresh signs of Bears in many places, but could not put one up. Chased a wolf half a mile without success. Returned well pleased with my day's work.

July 2ᵈ. Went to Princeton (40 miles) for letters. Met Messʳˢ. —— and ——, English visitors to our Prairie.

July 4ᵗʰ. Anniversary of independance. Last night I assisted in raising the flag of liberty in the public square, which this morning waved proudly over the group of young citizens assembled there to celebrate the day with festal games. The young men of the more respectable class gave a ball to all the damsels of the village and the vicinity. It commenced at three o'clock.

Some few of the girls were really handsome, and all were well dressed and appeared to be very happy. English country dances, or sets as they are called were attempted without success. In reels and cotillions they were quite at home.

In this land of equality it is very difficult to keep improper persons out of a public or even a private party. This evening some of the young men armed themselves with Dirks (poignards worn under the clothes) to resist the intrusion of the Militia, as the vulgar are contemptuously called. Unluckily one of our party was electioneering, and treated some hunters in the bar room with rum.

We supped in the open air at 7, and afterwards continued the dance till ten. After supper several attempts were made by some shabby looking fellows to come in, but they were prevented by the bar-keeper. The dancers kept it up most indefatigably, in spite of heat almost equal to that of the West Indies. In going away some of the gentlemen were insulted by the rabble, but the rumour that they were armed with dirks and pistols prevented serious mischief. In the night a large window was smashed to pieces, and the frame driven into the house.

The female part of the Company were all well dressed, but their birth and education as different as possible. The daughter of a proud and poor Virginian stood next the heiress of a bricklayer's fortune: An English adventurer danced with the wife of a member of the legislature; the maker of laws with the daughter of a lawless hunter: and a major of militia led out the only female servant in the inn, and who was obliged to leave the party to help, not her mistress but the tavern-keeper's wife, to set out the supper table.

July 5th. This day being Sunday was spent by the young men in visiting their mistresses and talking politics.

I am going tomorrow across the Wabash, and, probably, the next day I shall cross the Little Wabash to "hunt land."

Today the people of the Illinois meet to choose members of a convention to frame a constitution.

There will be a grand struggle between those who are for, and those who are against Slavery. Numbers are nearly balanced; but the advocates of Slaveholding gain strength daily.

Congress has granted to the people of the Illinois power to form a constitution, although there are but 35,000 inhabitants scattered over a tract 400 miles long and 200 miles wide. Congress has enlarged the limits of the state northwardly, so as to embrace 60 miles of the shore on the western side of Lake Michigan, and has given up the advantages to be drawn from its Salt works, which are the best in the United States. With these concessions it has forbidden Slavery, according to its Ordinance for the Government of the North Western Territory. But the people here are utterly regardless of ordinances, and will take the subject into their own hands, and say they will make a treaty with Congress as an independent State.

Liberty is the watchword of the popular or democratic party, and in their vocabulary it means any thing and every thing. It has no limits but the weakness of man, no boundary but that of his desires. To right oneself by violence, to oppose force to force, is reckoned a virtue here; and woe to the man who is suspected of cowardice.

If particular circumstances had not happened I should probably have gone up the Natchitoches or Red River on a trading expedition to the Osage Nation.[1] An honest little doctor of Princeton was

[1] Thomas Nuttall, during the course of his travels in the Arkan-

out last winter 600 miles up the Red River, and made a profitable trip of it. He likes the Country so well that he is going to take his young wife and infant, his father in law, and his wife's brothers and sister, with him, to settle on that remote frontier, 300 miles above the town of Natchitoches. I had almost engaged to go with an expert hunter and Indian trader, a second Drewyer or Clarke, when D^r. P—— told me of his plan. This seemed to add safety to enterprise; and we reckoned on engaging a large boat's crew to carry with us arms, beaver traps and Indian goods, and to make it a trading expedition on my part, a hunting one on J——'s, and to facilitate D^r. P—— to settle with his family. If I liked the adventure, I should return in the ensuing fall of the year, and buy the furs which J—— and P—— would by hunting and by barter be able to procure.

Our market would have been New Orleans or New York, according to circumstances. If New York, I should go there by sea from N. Orleans, purchase Indian fittings, take them by land to Pittsburg, thence down the Ohio, and the Mississippi, and up the Red River to our station on Pocoon point. . . .

Lax morals; few principles, but those deeply impressed on the mind; a careless haughtiness of manner, without any affectation, or consequential airs; and a quick perception of the ridiculous — these are

sas territory in 1819, visited the Red River country and the lands of the Osages. A good account may be found in his *Journal* (EARLY WESTERN TRAVELS, xiii, pp. 235-240, 245-262).

some of the characteristics of a man born and raised in the backwoods. The fondness for ridicule is remarkable in the Kentuckians, as well as their patience in taking a joke. But try to offend, and a knife or a dirk is drawn and aimed in an instant. Mʳ. S—— wears one, when among strangers, ten inches long in the blade. He is so avowedly fond of ridiculing unworthiness, that he confesses it is one of the greatest pleasures of his life, to laugh at and despise a scoundrel. — There is plenty of food for his spleen in this country.

Some of our Englishmen have won the Kindness of the Americans almost by surprise. G—— and Mʳ. B—— have both become favorites in a few days. A Kentuckian suspects nobody but a Yankee, whom he considers as a sort of Jesuit. An Englishman is one of that nation with whom he is proud to contend in the field of battle. Comes he as a visitor? he is received courteously; as a settler?— with frank hospitality and kindness. But if he thinks to flatter them by declaiming against his old country, he will be listened to with suspicion and contempt. You please them by openly avowing your affection and even your prejudice in favour of Old England, if you admit at the same time that you do not approve of all the acts of the British Government.

I fear you will find this a dull letter, but I am so racked with anxiety to see —— that I can attend to nothing. I must take my rifle and my horse and bury myself for another week in the forests with B——. He is a fine fellow. There are traits of kindness in his character, which soften down the sterner features of a ranger. Three Indians with their wives were killed at the South end of the English prairie 15 months ago. B—— had moved them off his hunting ground, but would not kill them, in pity of their wives. Three others 25 miles further off came after them, killed all six, and buried them in our Prairie. B—— said his hand should never be stained with woman's blood.

I have been at these hunters' cabins, and found them almost without food of any kind. A deer or a turkey has been brought in at nightfall; each has cut off the part he liked best, stuck it on a sharpened stick which he has inserted between the logs of the chimney, and so roasted it. The best skins and blankets have been chosen for me. The broken fiddle, and a cup of metheglin made of wild honey, have been produced; and dances, songs and mirth have lasted till past midnight. I have been obliged to get up and dance with them, such has been the intolerable noise. Living all together in one room, they have no notion that silence is necessary to a sleepy man: and, having no society and no regular engagements, night and day are alike to them.

The hunters on the Missouri are, I am told, a more abandoned set than those on the Wabash. They live entirely under the shelter of a blanket or the bark of trees, and are never nearer to each other than 9 or 10 miles, and moving every week or two. They trap a great many beavers and by this are enabled to buy spirits. They are more like the amphibious race on the banks of the Ohio, who are by turns hunters, boatmen, and farmers, and to whom robbing, violence and even murder, are familiar.

Instead of being more virtuous, as he is less refined, I am inclined to think that man's virtues are like the fruits of the earth, only excellent when subjected to culture. The force of this simile you will never feel, till you ride in these woods over wild strawberries, which die your horse's fetlocks like blood yet are insipid in flavour; till you have seen waggon loads of grapes, choked by the bramble and the poisonous vine; till you find peaches, tasteless as a turnip, and roses throwing their leaves of every shade upon the winds, with scarcely a scent upon them. Tis the hand of man that makes the wilderness shine. His footsteps must be found in the scene that is supremely & lastingly beautiful.

XVI

Princeton August 24. 1818.

You ask me, can a farmer with a capital of £250 live comfortably in this country? — Certainly much more comfortably than he can in England, if he has only £250, and no friends to lend him £2,000 in addition to it, or his friends are unwilling to help him. It is only a matter of choice then between servitude and independance. But there is no comfort here for the poor man beyond coarse food in plenty, coarse clothing, log huts, and the pleasure of repose earned by hard work. If the industrious farmer invest his capital in Land and Hogs in the Illinois, these will pay him 50 per cent, and that 25 per cent. per ann. for several succeeding years. But perhaps he must carry his horse-load of wheat 30 miles to the mill, — and his wife, if he have one, must make biscuits of it on his return. This is not consistent with English notions of comfort, but it is certain the backsettler is happier than the wretch, who is condemned to crouch to haughty landlords, to dread the oft repeated visit of the tytheman, the taxgatherer, and the overseer.

If a man can live within his income without losing his rank in society, and without being forced to borrow of those who think they oblige by lend-

ing; if he can pay the overwhelming taxes, which
the English Ministry have so thoughtlessly squan-
dered in making the English name hated to the
uttermost parts of the earth: there are in England
comforts, nay, sources of happiness, which will for
ages be denied to these half savage countries, good
houses, good roads, a mild and healthy climate,
healthy, because the country is old, society, the arts
of life carried almost to perfection, and Laws well
administered.

> " Blest he,— who dwells secure
> " Where Man, by Nature fierce, has laid aside
> " His fierceness; having learnt, though slow to learn,
> " The Manners and the Arts of civil life."

I will loosely classify English Emigrants, and
point out the sections of country, in which each
will find the greatest number of advantages.[1]

The English Country Gentleman, — may settle in
Virginia, district of Columbia, Maryland, New Jersey, and the lower part of Pennsylvania.

The genteel farmer — in Kentucky.

The rich yeoman — in Kentucky, Missouri, Tenessee, and Appalachicola.[2]

---

[1] Flint, in his *Letters from America,* gives an estimate of the comparative advantages offered to English emigrants by the several
sections of the United States (EARLY WESTERN TRAVELS, ix, pp. 181-
194). Fearon, in his *Sketches* (pp. 445-449), has an interesting
discussion of the classes of people whose betterment in America
could be reasonably assured, and who, therefore, should be en-
couraged to emigrate. These classes were (1) the extremely poor,
who could immediately change their state from that of paupers to
that of independent laborers; (2) mechanics whose income was
small and uncertain; and (3) small farmers having families to
support.

[2] By Appalachicola Fordham means the region in general about
the river of that name, between the southern boundary of Tennessee and the Gulf.

The poor farmer — with a capital of £300 & upwards, — in Illinois and Indiana.

Ditto, — if unmarried, — in Missouri, the lower parts of Kentucky and Appalouchia;[1] because in these countries he can have servants.

Mechanics, — if masters of the most useful trade, and capitalists, — always in the most settled parts of the Western Country, and generally in the Slave States.

Ditto — inferior workmen, — or without money, — in the new towns on the frontiers.

Engineers, smiths, founders, millwrights, and turners, may find employment in the larger towns on the Ohio.

Shopkeepers, and makers and dealers of articles of luxury, should never cross the mountains.

I cannot think that any elderly man, especially if he have a family delicately brought up, would live comfortably in a free state. In a slave State, if he have wealth, say, 5000£ and upwards, he may raise upon his own farm all the food and raiment, the latter manufactured at home, necessary to supply the wants of his own family.

This has been, till lately, the universal economy of the first Kentucky families. Thus, without living more expensively than in a free state, a family may have the comforts of domestic services, and yet find plenty of employment within doors; not sordid slavery that wears out the health, and depresses the

---

[1] Appalouchia was a name sometimes used in the early part of the last century to designate in a loose way the region now comprised in Oklahoma, Indian Territory, and eastern Texas.

spirits of Ohio, but useful yet light labours, that may be remitted and resumed at pleasure.

There is more difference between the manners of the female sex on the East and West sides of the Ohio River than on the East and West shores of the Atlantic Ocean. Servitude in any form is an evil, but the structure of civilized society is raised upon it. If the minds of women are left *unimproved*, their *morals* will be at the mercy of any man. It is much worse where there is no superior rank to influence them by example, or to awe them by disapprobation. I am conscious that I repeat again and again the same arguments — or rather I state similar facts; but it is an important subject.

Society may suffer more by the abjectness of Slaves than by the want of servants, and a father of a family would prefer to live where there are good free servants as in Europe, or where slaves have more liberty of action than servants, as in Kentucky. The question in these wildernesses is this: Shall we have civilization and refinement, or sordid manners and semi-barbarism, till time shall produce so much inequality of condition that the poor man must serve the rich man for his daily bread?

Messrs. F. and W. R—— arrived here yesterday. I go with them to-day to the prairies. . . .

XVII

Shawnee Oct. 17. 1818.

Soon after ——'s arrival at the prairie I fell sick,
and indeed throughout the Settlement there were
more sick than well. G—— had brought no medi-
cines with him and mine were almost all used or
given away, and the nearest Physician was thirty
miles off. My fever reduced me to a state of extreme weakness, but my nurse, by constantly sup-
plying me with corn meal gruel and chicken broth
prevented me from sinking under the violence of
my disorder.

The fever soon became a regular intermittent,
of which I was soon cured by bark and laudanum.

These intermittent fevers are the Scourges of
new Settlements in the Western Country. They
are seldom dangerous and are much under the power of medicine, but ought to be considered by Emigrants as unavoidable. When provided for, they
are slight and of little consequence.

The first year may be passed by a careful or ro-
bust person without receiving any injury from the
climate, but in the second the system becomes relaxed by heat. I cannot explain how, but I can
state the fact as related to me, and confirmed by
my own experience, that those who come from
Northern and healthy climates will in these South-

ern latitudes suffer a change of constitution, and that this change will be produced or accomplished by a fit of sickness. This is not to be wondered at, when we consider that for some weeks in the year the air is a perfect hot bath, and, for another period of equal duration the cold causes the quicksilver to sink 8°. below zero in Fahrenheit's Thermometer.

The Western Americans, especially the poorer class, are likewise very subject to febrile diseases. Their irregular way of living, their intemperance, the great mental excitement which to them is pleasure, produced by gambling, racing, fighting and moving, wear their constitutions. Their lean carcasses, their pale and eager countenances, early in life marked with wrinkles, and their reckless air, shew them to be adventurers, to whom anything is more welcome than plodding industry; to whom risk and danger is the preferable road to wealth, and the only path to honour. . . .

The leaves are now falling. We have fine delightful weather with frosty nights. The woods are beautifully[1] The Ohio is low. I have crossed it twice this morning, and never saw it look so calmly beautiful. The canoe scarcely left a ripple behind it and seemed to glide without impulse through the transparent stream.

The climate of the Illinois is more agreeable than that of England. The sky is brighter, the air more transparent, but at present, less healthy. The coun-

---

[1] The sentence stands thus incomplete in the manuscript.

try is intersected with innumerable streams whose overflowings produce swamps, which partially dry up in the summer, filling the air with mosquitoes and noxious effluvia. There are situations elevated and remote from stagnant waters, such as the English Prairie. But even here English Emigrants ought to expect to suffer a *seasoning,* before they can be inured to the changes of the weather. These changes are less sudden with us than in the state of Ohio, and become less and less so as we advance southward and southwestward, till in Appalouchie 500 miles west of the Mississippi, a climate is found of medium temperature; the summers being cooled by the breezes from the snowy mountains of Mexico, and the northern winds are tempered by passing over the Prairies of the Missouri.

You will take into consideration, that disorders of the lungs are here almost unknown, and that those who are already invalids are quite as likely to improve as to injure their constitutions by removing to this Country. I am more strong and healthy than I was in England, and I should probably have escaped the seasoning sickness, if the summer had not been uncommonly hot and wet. When good houses are erected, roads opened, and mills built, the health of the people will be much better. . . .

XVIII

The town of Albion planned — Continued surveying — The surrounding prairies — Prairie fires — Instructions for Emigrants: Capital required — Paying occupations — Clothing to be brought — Blankets a good investment — Travelling in the steerage — The journey from Philadelphia to Pittsburg — Down the Ohio to the Illinois Country.

English Prairie Oct. 30. 1818.

I AM laying off a new town to be called Albion.[1] It will consist of 8 streets and a public square. Most likely it will be the County Town, and if so, there will be a Court house and a gaol, as well as a Market house and a Chapel, which last will be built whether it be the seat of justice or not. I wished to have sent you a plan of this town, but I cannot spare the time. I have never been more busily employed in my life than I am now.

As soon as I have laid out this town, and the winter is well set in, I intend entering some more land, as the waters are up, and you may know what

---

[1] Albion became the town center of the English settlements and in 1821 it was made the seat of Albion County. It was situated in the northern portion of Flower's tract, two and a half miles east of Wanborough, the home of the Birkbecks. Welby, who visited the English Prairie in 1819, says of the town: "Notwithstanding the miserably unprovided state in which I found it, much had certainly been done, and more was rapidly doing towards rendering the place habitable. Among other well-judged resolutions, they had determined that in future all the houses should be substantially built of bricks, for the manufacture of which they have, as I understood, plenty of good clay in the neighborhood. A neat covered market, and place of worship . . . had been finished and opened to the public; to which I have to add that a roomy boarding house and tavern were half up; a store (shop) pretty well supplied was opened" (EARLY WESTERN TRAVELS, xii, p. 256). Woods (*Two Years' Residence*) tells us that in 1820 the town contained about twenty cabins in addition to the structures mentioned by Welby (EARLY WESTERN TRAVELS, x, p. 272). Fordham himself kept a store in Albion for some time before his return to England. There is an interesting account of the founding of the town in Flower's *History of the English Settlement in Edwards County, Illinois*, pp. 127-142.

15

places are acceptible or not, or what lands are too wet for cultivation or healthfulness; in short, you are sure not to be deceived by the apparent beauty of the situation.

I was yesterday taken from the New Town Survey to explore, and run the section lines over, the Long Prairie[1] and the Bon pas Prairie,[2] G—— not being able to make out the corner trees, and being besides too busy to leave home two days in succession.

I had never before crossed them so high from the mouth of the river, and was delighted with the beauty and variety of these meadows. The Bon Pas Prairie extends itself like a vast lake of verdure. The soil is rich, but lies rather too low.

The Northern arm of the Long Prairie is more like an immense river, studded with islands of wood, and bounded by dark forests, whose irregular outlines present to the eye fresh views at almost every step. The surface of this Prairie is gently undulating, completely free from brushwood, and its soil is still more rich than that of the Bon Pas Prairie. I have noted down some sections to enter for friends. . . .

Since I began to write this letter I have been interrupted by a tremendous fire in the Prairie, which driven by a strong South wind threatened our habitations. By the exertions of about 40 Americans

---

[1] The Long Prairie lay in Edwards County, about two miles east from the English Prairie. It was a strip nine miles in length (from north to south) and from one to one and a half in width.

[2] The Bonpas Prairie lay in Edwards County, four miles northeast of Albion. It was about two miles in diameter.

we saved every thing but a hay stack of G———'s.

It was the most glorious and most awful sight I ever beheld. A thousand acres of Prairie were in flames at once; — the sun was obscured, and the day was dark before the night came. The moon rose, and looked dim and red through the smoke, and the stars were hidden entirely. Yet it was still light upon the earth, which appeared covered with fire. The flames reached the forests, and rushed like torrents through. Some of the trees fell immediately, others stood like pillars of fire, casting forth sparkles of light. Their branches are strewed in smoking ruins around them.

While I was with G———'s people, burning a trough round his house, I saw the fire approach my own. It almost had surrounded it. I ran with my utmost speed, and found I could not get round the fire. A small opening appeared in one part, and I dashed through, though not without singing my hunting shirt and scorching my mocassins with the glowing ashes.

A small creek near my house stopped the fire; which, however, would not have reached it, as the grass had been eaten down and trodden to pieces by my horses. The way to stop the fire is to light smaller fires, which are kept from spreading by beating the grass with Clapboards or poles. This can only be effectual where the grass is short, or much trodden.

There are five large fires visible tonight, some many miles off.

The prairies are fired by the hunters to drive out the deer. Two or three years after a place is settled, the grass is eaten down and will not burn.

We have now 200 English on our Settlement.[1] Many are discontented; but the strong-minded regret that they did not come out sooner. . . .

* * *

[The following directions were given by the author to young men of small fortune in England who might feel inclined to emigrate.[2]]

If you are tired of a state of dependency, or if you are not in a good line of business, come out if you can raise 300£.

You need not work at any laborious employment, but you must not mind a little rough living at first. I would advise you to learn to butcher a hog, to cut it up, and to salt it down properly; likewise a bullock. For the most profitable trade is salting pork and beef for home consumption, or for New Orleans.

Dealing in corn, grain, and flour, pays extremely

___

[1] This was in October, 1818. Under date of August 16, 1819, Richard Flower wrote in his *Letters* that in a tract between the Great and Little Wabash seventeen miles from east to west and from four to six from north to south, where a year and a half before there had been but a few hunters' cabins, there were about 60 English families, comprising 400 souls, and 150 American families, aggregating 700 inhabitants (EARLY WESTERN TRAVELS, x, p. 104).

[2] A similar body of instructions was appended by Fearon to his *Sketches of America* (pp. 453-462). He gives advice regarding the choice of a vessel for the passage across the Atlantic, provisions to be carried by cabin and steerage passengers, clothing and other articles to be brought, and means of reaching the interior from the seaboard. His suggestions agree essentially with those here offered by Fordham.

well. There are indeed many things you could do here, and your choice would be puzzled with the variety.

Bring three good coats, cloth waistcoats and trowsers, for Breeches are never worn here, except by a few English; three or four pair of light linen trowsers; two suits of fustian coats and trowsers; and several pair of worsted and cotton socks, but no stockings. Bring no shooting jacket, unless you have it by you.

Let your chest be made of seasoned deal, and the lid should have a groove in three sides, and the box have a slip or tongue to fit into it. The back part should have a rule joint, like a table. Such a box would be air tight.

The only article of merchandise I can recommend you to bring is blankets; some tolerably good, others coarse. These will pay you Cent per Cent. Invest £50 in this article.

Come in the steerage, if there are but few steerage passengers, but don't venture among a great many; and by all means, take your passage in an American ship. If you can meet with two or three respectable young men, board yourselves, and you may live a little better than on ship provisions.

Do not bring with you any English rifles, or indeed any firearms but a pair of pistols. A good rifle gunlock would be valuable.

I will suppose you come by way of New York to Philadelphia. Bring with you, if you can procure them, letters of introduction; and at the latter city enter your intention of becoming a citizen of the United States.

Engage a waggoner to carry your box and bed; but not yourself. The inside of the waggon is always filled, so that you cannot ride with any comfort. Your ship mattress and blankets are the best things you can bring to sleep on. You may wrap them in a horse-rug, rolled up and fastened with two stirrup leathers. By sleeping on your own bed, you will save from 12½ to 25 cents per night, and avoid catching anything disagreeable.

You may perhaps meet with an intelligent, well-behaved, waggoner; this will add much to the comfort of your journey, and you may, by rendering him a little assistance now and then, make him your friend.

Americanise your appearance as much as you can; you will be treated better. You may pick up companions on the road, but beware lest you associate yourself with a scoundrel.

Address your luggage to some merchant at Pittsburg, and get a letter of credit sent forward to him. Otherwise, should you fall sick, or not choose to keep up with the waggon, you will then be under no uneasiness respecting it. One small trunk or portmanteau you should have with you to contain a change of linen.

Arrived at Pittsburg, you would take your passage to Cincinnati in a flat boat, or buy a skiff. Land at Evansville, leave your baggage there, and proceed to Princeton.

SELECTED LIST OF CONTEMPORARY TRAVELS

The following volumes are frequently cited in the introduction and notes by short titles. Complete titles are given below for the sake of reference.

Birkbeck (Morris), *Notes on a Journey in America from the Coast of Virginia to the Territory of Illinois, with Proposals for the Establishment of a Colony of English* (Philadelphia, 1817).

Birkbeck (Morris), *Letters from Illinois* (London, 1818).

Bradbury (John), *Travels in the Interior of America in the Years 1809, 1810, and 1811* (London, 1819). Reprinted in Thwaites, *Early Western Travels, 1748-1846: A series of annotated Reprints of some of the best and rarest contemporary volumes of travel descriptive of the aborigines and social and economic conditions in the middle and far West, during the period of early American settlement* (Cleveland, 1904); v.

Bullock (William), *Sketch of a Journey through the Western States of North America. With a description of Cincinnati, by B. Drake and E. D. Mansfield* (London, 1827). Thwaites, *Early Western Travels,* xix.

Buttrick (Tilly, Jr.), *Voyages, Travels, and Discoveries* (Boston, 1831). Thwaites, *Early Western Travels*, viii.

Cobbett (William), *A Year's Residence in the United States of America* (London, 1818).

Cuming (Fortescue), *Sketches of a Tour to the Western Country, through the States of Ohio and Kentucky* (Pittsburg, 1810). Thwaites, *Early Western Travels*, iv.

Evans (Estwick), *Pedestrious Tour of Four Thousand Miles, through the Western States and Territories* (Concord, N. H., 1819). Thwaites, *Early Western Travels*, viii.

Faux (William), *Memorable Days in America: being a Journal of a Tour to the United States, principally undertaken to ascertain, by positive evidence, the condition and probable prospects of British Emigrants; including accounts of Mr. Birkbeck's Settlement in the Illinois* (London, 1823). Thwaites, *Early Western Travels*, xi-xii.

Fearon (Henry Bradshaw), *Sketches of America. A Narrative of a Journey of five thousand miles through the Eastern and Western States of America* (London, 1818).

Flint (James), *Letters from America* (Edinburgh, 1822). Thwaites, *Early Western Travels*, ix.

Flower (Richard), *Letters from Lexington and the Illinois, containing a Brief Account of the English Settlement in the Latter Territory, and a Refutation of the Misrepresentations of Mr. Cob-*

bett (London, 1819). Thwaites, *Early Western Travels*, x.

Flower (Richard), *Letters from the Illinois, 1820, 1821. Containing an Account of the English Settlement at Albion and its Vicinity, and a Refutation of Various Misrepresentations: Those more particularly of Mr. Cobbett* (London, 1822). Thwaites, *Early Western Travels*, x.

Harris (Thaddeus M.), *Journal of a Tour into the Territory Northwest of the Alleghany Mountains, made in the Spring of the Year 1803* (Boston, 1805). Thwaites, *Early Western Travels*, iii.

Harris (William Tell), *Remarks made during a Tour through the United States of America during the Years 1817, 1818, and 1819* (London, 1821).

Hulme (Thomas), *Journal made during a Tour in the Western Countries of America: September 30, 1818-August 7, 1819.* Thwaites, *Early Western Travels*, x.

Melish (John), *Travels in the United States of America in the Years 1806 & 1807 and 1809, 1810 & 1811* (Philadelphia, 1812). Two vols.

Michaux (François André), *Voyage à l'ouest des Monts Alléghanys, dans les Etats de l'Ohio, et du Kentucky, et du Tennessée, et retour a Charleston par les Hautes-Carolines* (Paris, 1804). English edition (London, 1805). Thwaites, *Early Western Travels*, iii.

Nuttall (Thomas), *Journal of Travels into the Ar-*

kansa Territory, during the Year 1819, with Occasional Observations on the Manners of the Aborigines (Philadelphia, 1821). Thwaites, *Early Western Travels,* xiii.

Ogden (George W.), *Letters from the West, comprising a Tour through the Western Country, and a Residence of Two Summers in the States of Ohio and Kentucky* (New Bedford, 1823). Thwaites, *Early Western Travels,* xix.

Welby (Adlard), *Visit to North America and the English Settlements in Illinois, with a Winter Residence at Philadelphia* (London, 1821). Thwaites, *Early Western Travels,* xii.

Woods (John), *Two Years' Residence in the Settlement of the English Prairie, in the Illinois Country, United States* (London, 1822). Thwaites, *Early Western Travels,* x.

INDEX

Marietta, Fordham at, 86;
early history of, 86-87.
Maryland, physical features
of, 59; inhabitants of, 60.
Massie, Henry, 89.
Massie, Nathaniel, 92.
Maysville (Kentucky), Fordham at, 92; described by
travellers, 92.
Melish, John, investigations
in America, 70; publishes
his *Travels*, 70.
Michigan, Territory of, 101.
Middle West, early emigration to, 14-17; routes of
travel to, 52; classes of inhabitants, 124-127; Eastern
prejudice against, 131.
Missouri River, hunters on,
224.
Monroe, James, designates a
"seminary township" in
Indiana, 150.

NANTUCKET, people of de-
scribed, 196.
New Albany, founding of,
157; Fordham at, 158.
New Harmony, Fordham at,
205; establishment of, 205;
life of inhabitants, 206-208;
religious services, 208.
New Orleans, trade from
Pittsburg to, 75-76.
"New Orleans," launched, 15.
Newport (Kentucky), found-
ing of, 164.
New York, arrival of British
immigrants at, 21.
Norfolk, Fordham at, 51.
Northwest Ordinance, enact-
ed, 86.
Northwest Territory, divided
by Congress, 112; slavery
in, 194.
Nuttall, Thomas, visit to
Pittsburg, 76.

OGDEN, George W., publishes his *Letters*, 28.
O'Hara, General James, 76.

Ohio Company, organization
of, 86.
Ohio, increase in population
of, 14.
Ohio River, methods of navigating, 53; craft described
by Evans, 79-80; narratives
of navigation, 80; descent
of by Fordham, 81; the
"falls" of, 105; aspects of,
184, 187-188; La Salle on,
188.
Owen, Robert, at New Har-
mony, 206.

PARLIAMENT, demand for
reform of, 18; enacts the
Corn Law, 18.
Paroquets, abundant in the
Ohio Valley, 138.
Patoka River, described, 137;
Fordham descends, 138-139.
Pell, Gilbert, anti-slavery
leader in Illinois, 210.
Pennsylvania, the people of,
60, 64-66.
Pennsylvania Road, 59.
Petapsco River, 58.
Petersburg (Virginia), des-
cribed by Fordham and by
Birkbeck, 48.
Piankeshaw Indians, 115.
Pike, Zebulon, western trav-
els of, 123.
Pitt, Fort, 55, 73.
Pittsburg, plan of drawn by
Fordham, 74; early history
of, 71; described by trav-
ellers, 72; commercial con-
ditions at, 75; dependence
on the Ohio River trade, 76.
Pittsburg Pike, 59.
Pontchartrain, Fort, 146.
Pope, Nathaniel, territorial
delegate of Illinois, 175.
Population, increase of, in
Middle West, 14.
Portsmouth (Ohio), Fordham
at, 90.